"Brent Crowe has done it again ... on how our God-given imagina... tone existence to living life in t... Mac Genius who teaches you how to maximize an instrument you already own, *Reimagine* takes us step-by-step through a tutorial that unlocks a new level of faith."

— DAVID NASSER, pastor, Christ City Church, Birmingham, Alabama; author and speaker

"What a daring and much-needed book! Brent Crowe has clearly articulated a road map on how to use our God-given gift of imagination so that every Christ follower can live a story that reflects God's grand narrative. *Reimagine* will liberate your thinking and could very possibly transform the trajectory of your future."

— PAT WILLIAMS, senior vice president, the Orlando Magic; author of *Leadership Excellence*

"Brent invites us to take a deep look at ourselves and the world around us and to ask what role we each can play to reimagine the world as God intended it. This book is a game changer for those who take it to heart."

— SEAN MCDOWELL, educator and speaker; author of *Ethix: Being Bold in a Whatever World*

"Brent Crowe's ability to communicate is compelling. *Reimagine* nourishes starved minds and energizes lethargic hearts to a fresh way of understanding God's Word and world. It is a call to all Christians to utilize the creativity God gave us to speak truth to a culture that so desperately needs hope. A super book!"

— WILLIAM E. BROWN, PhD, president, Cedarville University

"Combining theological truth with stirring slices of life, Brent helps us unpack what it looks like to engage the imagination in seeing God's will done on earth as it is in heaven. Prepare to dig deep and allow God to stretch your imagination further than it's gone before!"

— MICHAEL CATT, senior pastor, Sherwood Baptist Church, Albany, Georgia; executive producer, Sherwood Pictures

"Walk through God's story of redemption with fresh young eyes. It will broaden your view of his plan."

—DR. JOHNNY HUNT, senior pastor, First Baptist Church, Woodstock, Georgia; former president, Southern Baptist Convention

"What the world would look like if God got his way is a strong statement that starts *Reimagine*. This is something we should all think about, and Brent ponders it in a sound theological way. I personally was challenged in my thought process and in my walk with Christ while reading this book."

—BRIAN MILLS, youth pastor, Long Hollow Baptist Church, Hendersonville, Tennessee; coauthor of *Checkpoints*

"Brent masterfully demonstrates how Christians walking in the Spirit can practically perform God's agenda. *Reimagine* is a must-read for anyone struggling with what it means to know and do the will of God."

—MIKE CALHOUN, vice president, Word of Life Fellowship; author of *Where Was God When . . . ?*

"*Reimagine* is a powerfully insightful book that explores God's plan for humanity and the reality of where humanity is. Through Scripture, Brent Crowe takes a profound look at how Christ followers are instrumental in carrying out God's will. You will be challenged and inspired to be part of his redemptive plan for mankind!"

—JEFF BORTON, coauthor of *Simple Student Ministry*; pastor of students, Christ Fellowship, Miami, Florida

"We have all been given the gift of imagination. That gift comes from the most creative designer ever: God. *Reimagine* will open your mind to a new way of thinking and help you be proactive and not reactive to everyday issues."

—SHAUN BLAKENEY, next generation pastor, Christ Fellowship Church, West Palm Beach, Florida

REIMAGINE

**what the world would look
like if God got his way**

BRENT CROWE

NavPress
Discipleship Inside Out®

Discipleship Inside Out®

NavPress is the publishing ministry of The Navigators, an international Christian organization and leader in personal spiritual development. NavPress is committed to helping people grow spiritually and enjoy lives of meaning and hope through personal and group resources that are biblically rooted, culturally relevant, and highly practical.

For a free catalog go to www.NavPress.com or call 1.800.366.7788 in the United States or 1.800.839.4769 in Canada.

ISBN-13: 978-1-61291-354-4

Cover design by Arvid Wallen

Some of the anecdotal illustrations in this book are true to life and are included with the permission of the persons involved. All other illustrations are composites of real situations, and any resemblance to people living or dead is coincidental.

Unless otherwise identified, all Scripture quotations in this publication are taken from The Holy Bible, English Standard Version (ESV), copyright © 2001 by Crossway Bibles, a division of Good News Publishers. Used by permission. All rights reserved. Other versions used include: THE MESSAGE (MSG). Copyright © 1993, 1994, 1995, 1996, 2000, 2001, 2002. Used by permission of NavPress Publishing Group; the New King James Version (NKJV). Copyright © 1982 by Thomas Nelson, Inc. Used by permission. All rights reserved; and the Holy Bible, New International Version® (NIV®), Copyright © 1973, 1978, 1984 by Biblica, used by permission of Zondervan, all rights reserved.

Crowe, Brent, 1978-
  Reimagine what the world would look like if God got his way / Brent Crowe.
    p. cm.
  Includes bibliographical references.
  ISBN 978-1-61291-354-4
  1. Christian life. 2. Imagination—Religious aspects—Christianity.
3. Redemption—Christianity. I. Title.
  BV4501.3.C767 2013
  248.4–dc23

                         2012034747

Printed in the United States of America

2 3 4 5 6 7 8 / 18 17 16 15 14 13

This book is dedicated to my children:
Gabriel, Charis, and Mercy

Serving as your father has been the classroom for me to learn
volumes on the God-given gift of imagination. This book is also
dedicated to the children not yet in our home but already in our
hearts. We are imagining a day when our family will be complete.

CONTENTS

REDEMPTIVE IMAGINATION AND THE TWO WILLS OF GOD

B y the time she was able to escape the imprisonment of shock that had held her hostage for over an hour, she reached for her phone in a desperate attempt to cry out for help. It was four o'clock in the morning, and in many ways the last ninety minutes had been a blur.

Somewhere around 2:00 a.m. she heard the sound of breaking glass toward the front of her one-bedroom, ground-level apartment. With her heart pounding out of her chest, she sat up, but by then a shadowy figure was looming over her with gun in hand. Her first thought was a prayer, *Please don't let my little boy wake up. God, please don't let him get hurt.* Time seemed to slow down as the gunman shouted and cursed, demanding money.

Boy, has he come to the wrong house, she thought. She was a single mom in debt up to her eyeballs, trying to overcome addiction and ten years of bad choices, all while raising her son. There wasn't even enough money to furnish six hundred square feet—not even enough to buy a crib for her son, who was at this very moment resting next to her in bed, unaware of the imminent danger. Paralyzed by panic, she couldn't speak, frustrating the intruder as he kicked around what few possessions she had.

This went on for thirty minutes: he kicked and threw things, like a child not getting his way; she sat and stared, hoping to God her son would emerge from this unscathed.

Finally the faceless gunman exited, and there she sat in shock and fear, wondering if the whole ordeal was actually concluded. When she was finally able to reach for her phone, she called the one person most twentysomething women would like to call: her dad. Much to her disappointment, her father was unmoved by her tale of tragedy. For him this was simply one in a long history of ordeals. He had bailed her out more times than he could count, and she had lied and cried so many times that he was out of patience.

She got off the phone, torn between disbelief and sobering reality, and contemplated her next call. There was a family she had grown close to; they had helped her out on many occasions, watching her son while she worked and helping her put groceries in the fridge. Unfortunately, they were out of town, but they had taken her to their church, itself in its infancy with roughly thirty members and only a year old. The pastor and his wife had given her their home number, encouraging her to call if she ever needed any help. Scared, lonely, estranged from her family, and at the end of her rope, she decided to take the pastor and his wife up on their offer.

By the time the sun rose, most of this little community of Christ followers had gathered at her little apartment. By the time the sun went down that night, her fear had been replaced with security and her loneliness with community. Though her family would have nothing to do with her—after all, she was a lying, thieving, promiscuous drug addict—she felt as if she had the beginnings of a new family. The church had moved her from the ground-level apartment to one on the third floor and had added two extra locks, some used furniture, food in the fridge, and a crib for her son. What evil and sin had destroyed, goodness and obedience to the faith had restored.

« • »

In the story above, a single mom was born into a family who loved her (though that love carried certain limitations) and wanted her to do well. However, she listened to the wrong voice—as did Adam and Eve in the garden—and thus heard the wrong question.

Did God really say . . .

- Don't rebel against your parents?
- Don't be under the influence of drugs and alcohol?
- Don't live a promiscuous life?
- Don't lie?
- Don't steal?

The answer is yes on every count:

- Honor your father and mother. (Exodus 20:12)
- Do not be drunk with wine. (Ephesians 5:18)

- Flee sexual immorality. (1 Corinthians 6:18)
- Do not lie to one another. (Colossians 3:9)
- You shall not steal. (Exodus 20:15)

Yet even though she listened to the wrong voice, as we all have, that didn't keep the Father from asking as to her whereabouts, as if he didn't already know, and sending Jesus to save her. I would suggest that God did not want her to have a child out of wedlock, become addicted to drugs, rebel against her parents, lie, and steal. He wanted something different for her, but God didn't get his way for two reasons: her sin and the sin of those around her. This leads us to the central question that will in turn lead to the core idea of this book.

Does God always get his way? I ask that as someone who is as conservative in my theology as Dr. Billy Graham. I believe God is sovereign. By sovereign, I affirm God's power and rule over his creation. I agree with theologian Dr. Wayne Grudem as he defines God's omnipotence and sovereignty to mean "God is able to do all his holy will. . . . God's exercise of power over his creation is also called God's *sovereignty.*" Furthermore, "we exercise choice and make real decisions regarding the events of our lives. Although our will is not absolutely free in the way God's is, God has nonetheless given us *relative freedom* within our spheres of activity in the universe he has created."[1] In other words, "The LORD has established his throne in the heavens, and his kingdom rules over all" (Psalm 103:19).

So with that in mind, let's ask again: Does God always get his way? The question itself may be a bit alarming, but consider this our starting point. God has two wills, a *decreed* or hidden will and a *desired* or revealed will. This doesn't mean God is suffering from some form of divine schizophrenia. It means there is that which God has *determined* and that which he *desires* to happen. The idea that God has two wills has been affirmed over the last 250-plus years by such Christian leaders as Jonathan Edwards in the 1700s and John Piper in the present day. Piper has written,

> Affirming the will of God to save *all*, while also affirming the unconditional election of *some*, implies that there are at least "two wills" in God, or two ways of willing. It implies that God decrees one state of affairs while also willing and teaching that a different state of affairs should come to pass. This distinction in the way God wills has been expressed in various ways throughout the centuries. It is not a new contrivance. For example, theologians have spoken of sovereign will and moral will, efficient will and permissive will, secret will and revealed will, will of decree and will of command, decretive will and preceptive will, *voluntas signi* (will of sign) and *voluntas beneplaciti* (will of good pleasure), etc.[2]

Theologian Dr. Daniel Akin puts it this way:

> To simplify this profound truth we might say it like this, "God is *willing* to save all though He does not *will* to save all, He *desires* the salvation of all but did not *decree* the salvation of all. God *delights* in the eternal perishing of no one, though He has *designed* a world where some do perish eternally. Thus we distinguish between what God would like to see happen and what He has designed will happen.[3]

If you think it sounds like a mystery, you are correct. Furthermore — and this should really bake your noodle — if it sounds like a mystery the human mind will never exhaustively understand, you are absolutely correct. The question, then, becomes, Is there room in your life and view of God for mystery? I certainly hope there is, as God cannot be contained and has never fit into anyone's box or system. You can study him systematically, realizing the system itself will inevitably have limitations—because God has not given us a system or textbook, but rather has told us a story. The Bible itself is the true story of the world, and we have the sacred opportunity to enter and be a part of his story. Within that story we are confronted with the tale of a hero God, redeeming his people and defeating evil. C. S. Lewis said, "The heart of Christianity is a myth which is also a fact. . . . By becoming fact it does not cease to be myth: that is the miracle."[4]

Stepping into God's grand narrative reveals to us that God has some desires or wants. We know what God wants because he has revealed it; on the other hand, we don't know what God has decreed because it is hidden. To believe we are to know his decreed will is to somehow play a cosmic game of Go Fish in which we are trying to guess what cards God is holding. The very thought of this is ridiculous.

Thus, let me pose another question: Should we learn to live and act based on God's revealed desires or will? I hope the answer is obvious in the way the question is framed, making the central question of this book all the more relevant: *What would it look like if God got his way?*

The astounding thing is that we get to answer that question by using our imagination, a gift that has long been forgotten or neglected, to respond to his revealed desires by being obedient to the faith. It's not that God is dependent upon us. God wasn't dependent upon Adam to name the animals, yet he allowed him to use his imagination to accomplish this task. God has never been backed into a corner, hoping humans will come through; rather, he allows us to be part of the solution.

So what are a few of God's wants or desires?

- God wants us to care for the obviously overlooked. (Matthew 25:35-40)
- God wants people to be in healthy relationships. (Ecclesiastes 4:9-12)
- God wants orphans to find families (or families to find orphans). (James 1:27)
- God wants marriages that are strong, in which divorce isn't an option. (Genesis 2:23-24; 1 Corinthians 7:10-11)
- God wants people to go to heaven. (1 Timothy 2:3-4)
- God wants people to be in healthy, Christ-centered community. (Romans 14:15)
- God wants people to love and not hate. (Matthew 22:37-40)
- God wants people to be delivered from poverty. (Proverbs 3:9-10)
- God wants people to be free from addiction. (1 Corinthians 6:12)
- God wants disease eradicated. (Matthew 8:14-17; Revelation 21:4)
- God wants people to have a healthy understanding of their sexuality. (Genesis 19:1-13; Leviticus 18:22; 20:13; Romans 1:18-32; 1 Corinthians 6:9-10; 1 Timothy 1:8-11)
- God wants the bully to be confronted and the victim to be protected. (Luke 10:27; Micah 6:8)
- God wants families to be whole and for abuse to never enter the picture. (Ephesians 5:22-33)

- God wants single moms to find hope. (Jeremiah 29:11; 1 Corinthians 15:19)
- God wants men to define *man* according to his Word. (Colossians 3:18-21; 1 Peter 3:7)

God wants an awful lot.

But will God get what he wants? Or maybe our question could be better stated like this: Will God get what he wants for your life? Remember, we get to answer this question and others like it by reimagining our lives and what God surely wants for us. In the coming chapters, I'll paint a picture of this redemptive imagination and all that it can accomplish.

I believe God is in charge of his creation and that he has the right to rule and overrule. But at the same time, there is a tension that exists within his creation—because it is fallen.

And why is it fallen? Simply put, God gave humans freedom and the gift of choice. When God put Adam in the garden to "work it and keep it" his first instruction to him was, "And the LORD God commanded the man, saying, 'You may surely eat of every tree of the garden, but of the tree of the knowledge of good and evil you shall not eat, for in the day that you eat of it you shall surely die'" (Genesis 2:16-17). In my book *Chasing Elephants,* I examine the boundaries God established for Adam's freedom in the garden:

- A **respect** for the authority of God's words: "And the Lord God commanded the man."
- A **responsibility** to stay within the boundaries outlined by the words of God: "You may surely eat of every tree of the garden, but of the tree of the knowledge of good and evil you shall not eat."

- **Consequences** for crossing the stated boundaries: "In the day that you eat of it you shall surely die."

Unfortunately, that freedom was mishandled, resulting in what has historically been called the fall of man. It is important to point out that prior to this fall, the tension did not exist; Adam and Eve enjoyed a perfect relationship with God, and all of his creation existed in perfect harmony. In short, before the fall of man, we have a picture of what this world looks like when God gets his way (which will be further explored in the next chapter).

The fall of man can be understood as the tale of two questions. The first question is asked by the Enemy, the Devil: "Did God really say . . . ?" The second question is asked by God himself: "Adam, where are you?" Both, in fact, are leading questions. The answers are obvious. The Devil's question leads to rebellion, the Fall, or the de-creation of what God has established. The Father's question leads to redemption and the promise of Jesus (Genesis 3:15), or the re-creation of a relationship with God. This dichotomy also helps us understand how God is sovereign and at the same time doesn't always get his way. And of course this tension, in part, causes us to wrestle with what the world would look like if God got his way.

In this book we will be focusing on issues that face the family, the church, and the culture. Much can be gleaned from the Reformer Martin Luther's perspective on calling and the Christian. Luther, you may remember, was a central figure in one of the more important movements in Christian history: the Protestant Reformation, during which Protestants broke from the Catholic Church, which at that time (1517) was the one worldwide, established church of Christianity.

The central theme of the Reformation Luther helped lead was responsibility to and recognition of the authority of the Bible, articulated in his famous rallying cry *Sola Scriptora*, meaning "by Scripture alone." Out of this doctrine emerged an emphasis on "the priesthood of all believers," which helped the public at large see a sense of sacredness to their everyday comings and goings. God was no longer accessible only through a priest at a designated location (that is, church). Instead, every believer had access to God at every moment of every day. As you can imagine, this access fundamentally impacted the way people lived their lives. They no longer entered into the presence of God — they lived in the presence of God.

As a result, all of life now had a sense of *calling* attached to it. Being a parent or a sibling or a spouse or a baker or a doctor or a salesman was now lived out before the audience of God. In his book *God at Work*, Gene Edward Veith Jr. describes it this way: "'The priesthood of all believers' did not make everyone into church workers; rather, it turned every kind of work into a sacred calling."[5] Luther's understanding was that one lived with a multiplicity of callings on his life at any given time. Those callings emphasized one's role as a member of a church, culture, and family.

Using Luther's understanding of a multiplicity of callings as a rough template, *Reimagine* will examine some of the more disturbing trends affecting the church, family, and culture. My hope is to equip and encourage, so that as Christians we would be a people who do much more than articulate and expound upon the problem. We would be a people who instead apply grace-filled creativity, based on the foundation of Scripture, to situations empty of God's grace. My prayer is that we would not be the knee-jerk–reaction kind of Christians who say, "Well, they got what they deserved." *God, let us be those who drop to our knees, asking and imagining how we can be part of the solution.*

I'm going to offer a few imaginary thoughts (about real issues) in response to what the world would look like if God got his way. I believe this question — about a world vastly different from the one that currently exists — gives sacred relevance to our sanctification, though to some it may sound a bit heretical or unspiritual.

If you don't agree with me, just walk through any orphanage in the world where children don't even have the will to cry. Walk in, stand, observe, and hear the piercing sound of silence. Then ask yourself, *Is this what God wants?*

The world is full of pain, hurt, loneliness, and abuse. It is all around us, and I can't help but wonder if our inundation in it has caused our imaginations to go dormant and our hearts to grow calloused. I choose to believe (based on what the Bible teaches) God actually wants as many as possible to find peace, fulfillment, significance, and the way in him. I choose to believe God can get his way on this little blue marble called Planet Earth, but it will only happen when and where the movement of Christianity intersects with pain, hurt, loneliness, and abuse.

« • »

Reimagine is not an exhaustive treatment of any one issue plaguing the world today. Instead, I propose to use a redemptive imagination — a way to dreamcast a better world, one in which Christians act as God's agents to provide redemptive compassion and the love of Christ. We can *imagine* what it would be like if we solved any number of issues facing the family, the church, and the culture—and then we can *act* on it.

The first four chapters of *Reimagine* unpack the idea of imagination. First, we will seek the Scriptures in an effort to articulate a theology of imagination, thus laying a foundation for the thoughts that follow. Next, attention will be given to the role imagination has played in impacting the trajectory of history by analyzing a few key events. Third, we will explore the intellectual realities or convictions that will yield mental readiness to embrace and navigate your imaginary thoughts about real things. Finally, chapter 4 focuses on the fruit of a redemptive imagination—a dream that can be actualized.

The second half of *Reimagine* is designed to provide short stories or narratives that enable us to view either a redemptive imagination at work or a real-life scenario about which we could imagine a different and better way. Following each chapter are discussion questions to help you think about the stories and a redemptive imagination on a deeper level. Let each chapter serve as an experiment for the laboratory of the imagination—the brain. Put yourself into the characters and wrestle with the process of reimagining for the glory of God.

Finally, as you grapple with the message of this book, do so with an open mind and a willingness to discover a new way of thinking. The reason for this is significantly profound. You see, God has gotten his way before, and God will get his way again—but what would happen if God got his way in your life now? What a story that would be!

PART I

DISCOVERING A REDEMPTIVE IMAGINATION

CHAPTER 1

IMAGINOLOGY:
The Scaffolding for Imaginary Thoughts

The Christian is the one whose imagination should fly beyond the stars.
— Francis A. Schaeffer, *Art and the Bible*

We all have to some degree the power to imagine. This gift enables us to see meanings in material objects, to observe similarities between things which at first appear wholly unlike each other. It permits us to know that which the senses can never tell us, for by it we are able to see through sense impressions to the reality that lies behind things.
— A. W. Tozer, *Born After Midnight*

The world becomes a strange, mad, painful place, and life in it a disappointing and unpleasant business, for those who do not know about God. Disregard the study of God, and you sentence yourself to stumble and blunder through life blindfolded, as it were, with no sense of direction and no understanding of what surrounds you.
— J. I. Packer, *Knowing God*

One of the great privileges of my life was meeting the late Dr. Bill Bright. Dr. Bright is most well known for cofounding Campus Crusade for Christ, which, at the time of his death in 2003, was "the world's largest Christian ministry, [serving] people in 191 countries through a staff of 26,000 full-time employees and more than 225,000 trained volunteers working in some 60 niche ministries and projects ranging from military ministry to inner city ministry," according to the Bill Bright website. The booklet Bright wrote in 1956, *The Four Spiritual Laws*, "has been printed in some 200 languages and distributed to more than 2.5 billion people, making it the most widely disseminated religious booklet in history." His 1979 film, *Jesus*, "a feature-length documentary on the life of Christ . . . has been viewed by more than 5.1 billion people in 234 countries and has become the most widely viewed, as well as the most widely translated, film in history (786 languages)."[1] For nearly five decades, Dr. Bright had a laser-like focus on the Great Commission and presenting the love and claims of Christ to every living person on earth.

I will never forget the afternoon I was able to spend in conversation with this giant of the faith. It was obvious that his physical health was fast fading; he had been diagnosed a year earlier with pulmonary fibrosis. At the time, this disease had left him with only 40 percent use of his lungs. With oxygen feeding constantly through a tube into his nose and only months to live, he was nevertheless a portrait of spiritual strength. There wasn't a hint of disappointment or worry, only joy and satisfaction.

I went to school that afternoon at the feet of one who had run the race and kept his eyes on Jesus. When the afternoon had come to completion, I asked one final question: "Dr. Bright, if you could give one piece of advice to a young man just starting out in his journey of serving God, what would it be?" He answered the question and then wrote the answer on the inside cover of his book *God: Discover His Character*, "To Chris and Brent, One's view of God determines everything about us — With Christ's great love, Bill Bright 1 Cor. 13; Mt. 28:18-20."

Such simple words that for the last ten years have been etched on the tablet of my mind and heart. My view and understanding of God fundamentally determine everything about my life. I also find it fascinating that the book Dr. Bright was working on when he died was titled *Discover the Book God Wrote*, a book about understanding the Bible (although he would go Home before the final edits were even completed). There is an important connection between one's view of God and one's understanding of the Bible. A healthy view of God is thus determined by a healthy view of God's Word.

How is this relevant to a conversation about imagination? The foundation and filter for a redemptive imagination must be God's truth. The logic can be understood as follows:

- A proper understanding of Scripture will help produce an accurate view of God.
- An accurate view of God will inform a truthful view of what God wants.
- What God wants is to be the end goal of our imaginary thoughts.

These ideas lead us to the need to have a theology of imagination, or what we will refer to as *imaginology*.

THEOLOGY

The Christian should not be afraid of the word *theology*. It can be easily broken down into two Greek words: *theos* (God) and *logos* (word). Theology, in its most basic definition, is, therefore, words about or the study of God. In essence, a theology of *fill in the blank* is asking the question, What does God say about salvation . . . Christ . . . the church . . . the Holy Spirit . . . and so on?

In this conversation, we are seeking the answer to the question, How does theology shape and inform my thinking on imagination? The answer to this question will produce a theology of imagination that, in turn, affords our lives the ability to answer the all-important question, What would the world look like if God got his way?

Notice the role application plays in theology. Theology is not simply an experiment of the mind, it is an experiment with your life. In his modern-day classic *Knowing God*, J. I. Packer wrote concerning the role of theology, "In fact, however, it is the most practical project anyone can engage in. Knowing about God is crucially important for the living of our lives."[2] Application thus plays a fundamental role in pursuing theology. It is not something to be merely cognitively grasped; rather, it is to be experienced. If it is not experienced or lived out, then the pursuit is incomplete. In short, theology divorced from real living isn't good theology.

Now that it is understood that the core of theology is studying God, it may be helpful to think of theology as an ocean. The ocean can be experienced in a variety of ways. When I take my children to the beach, they usually like to play in the sand at the water's edge. They will build sand castles, collect shells, and chase the little waves as they roll in and then out. Occasionally one of them will work up the courage to venture into knee-deep water and square off with a mighty wave or two. It is quite entertaining to watch it all unfold because their experience is full, and yet they haven't even begun to experience the vastness of the ocean.

Scuba divers, on the other hand, experience the ocean differently. They take a boat out, usually to predetermined coordinates, and dive down with oxygen tanks that allow them to stay submerged for an extended period of time. They experience the ocean far differently than a child on the beach; it's an entirely different world underneath the sea. They see more than the child on the beach but still operate within human limitations.

Theology, then, is the exploration and study of God; to the kid on the beach or the experienced scuba diver in the sea, it offers a full experience. But God is God and we are his created beings — and as such, we can never fully experience or exhaust our study of God. Theology can be studied systematically, philosophically, historically, and practically, and with each approach we can but scratch the surface to the vastness of God. In short, our study can seek but never contain God. He cannot fit into a human box.

With that in mind, there are four sources for theology, according to world-renowned theologian Alister E. McGrath: Scripture, tradition, reason, and experience.[3] Of course, when McGrath refers to *Scripture* he is referring to the body of texts known as the Holy Bible that are "authoritative for Christian thinking."[4] By *tradition* he is referring to "a continuous stream of Christian teaching, life, and interpretation that can be traced from the time of the apostles."[5] Tradition focuses on continuity in thought and/or action demonstrated by the church throughout history (the rise and fall of Christian imagination will be examined in the next chapter). *Reason* refers to the fact that human beings are rational creatures, which makes the Christian faith rational. Reason supports the ideas of the Christian faith without limiting Christianity to what can be ascertained by reason.[6] For the purposes of our discussion, this is our rational ability to conceive a different way of doing things, that is, imagination. The final source for theology is *experience* or, more specifically, religious experience. The word *experience* is derived from the Latin word *experiential*, meaning "that which arises out of traveling through life."[7] Experience is what you learn through living. When someone says he has firsthand knowledge, it means he experienced something personally. Reason and experience are described and illustrated through stories in part 2; here the emphasis will be on Scripture and tradition.

THE SUPREME NORM: SCRIPTURE

Although each of the four sources for theology (Scripture, tradition, reason, experience) would be considered a primary source, Scripture should be considered the most primary of the four. In other words, where there is a contradiction or conflict among sources, the reality portrayed and framed by the Word is the "supreme norm."[8] So how does the Word of God inform our thinking in such a way that our imaginations can be used to glorify him?

The Bible can be understood as a grand narrative of reimagination and thus a great case study on the subject. Inside this narrative, we discover the beauty of God and his redemptive plan. To become captivated by God's beauty as it is demonstrated in his story is where a theology of imagination begins. But first, what does a "grand biblical narrative" mean? My friend Dr. Bruce Ashford has articulated well the four plot movements of the biblical narrative—creation, fall, redemption, and restoration:

> In creation [plot movement 1], we learn that this world is a created world made by the uncreated triune God, a good world that God intends to fill with people made in his image whom he will make a kingdom of priests. God's world is a world that reflects his glory and

points continually to the beauty and goodness of the Creator. In the fall [plot movement 2], however, man and woman rebelled against God and in doing so alienated themselves from him, from each other, from themselves, and from the rest of the created order. As a result, God's good creation is marred by the ugliness of sin, and that sin has a far broader impact than we might typically imagine. In redemption [plot movement 3], we see God's response to sin and rebellion. We learn that following man's rebellion, God promises to send One through whom he will redeem the nations and the world. The whole of Scripture speaks of this One, the Messiah, and the salvation he accomplished. The biblical narrative concludes with the restoration [plot movement 4] of the world God made, the establishment of the new heavens and new earth, foretold in the prophets, and inhabited by the redeemed of the nations who dwell eternally with their God.[9]

The significance of this, demonstrating the wisdom of God, is that story resonates best with the way the human mind works. "We think in pictures even though we speak and write with words," says Warren Wiersbe.[10] He quotes W. Macneile Dixon, who said, "The human mind is not . . . a debating hall, but a picture gallery."[11] In short, God has told a story, a *true* story. Because of the elements and plot movements within God's narrative, all other stories then make sense. We know who the bad guy is because we know who the enemy is in God's story — we know the hero must fall and rise again because God sent Jesus to die on the cross for our sins and rise again, making salvation possible. We live within the context of this. We were created perfect but needy; next, we rebelled — resulting in the need to be rescued and ultimately restored. Therefore, it only makes sense that the human mind resonates best with narratives.

Because of the story God has told, all other stories, including the tales of our lives, have meaning. Brian Godawa, a Christian who wrote the screenplay for the movie *To End All Wars*, states, "We are creatures of story, created by a storytelling God, who created the very fabric of our reality in terms of his story. Rather than seeing our existence as a series of unconnected random events without purpose, storytelling brings meaning to our lives through the analogy of carefully crafted plot that reflects the loving sovereignty of the God of the Bible."[12]

Furthermore, Jesus' primary means of communication was to tell parables or stories. His reason for doing this was twofold; first, his listeners would find themselves experiencing the story, imagining themselves within the anecdote he was telling, and thus experiencing the primary truth that he was teaching. Second, Jesus told stories because they were memorable and could be retold by his listeners.

The following are *thoughts from the plots* that will serve as scaffolding for an *imaginology*. As you consider these thoughts, notice God has his way in plot movement 1 (creation) and will once again, both exhaustively and ultimately, have his way with plot movement 4 (restoration). Yet presently we find ourselves living somewhere between these two.

We live in a fallen world that needs to recognize the redemption offered in the sacrificial love of Jesus; the reason God's will and way are not being upheld or even sought after in this fallen world has to do with the mismanagement of the gift of choice, as discussed in the introduction. I am not saying humans can in any way bring about the new heavens and new earth. But in light of a broken world that is *not* a portrait of God getting his way, how can we reimagine everything for the glory of God? Much of the answer will derive from these thoughts from the plots.

PLOT MOVEMENT 1: OBSERVATIONS FROM CREATION

Thought 1: "You were created in the image of God, created by an imaginative God who is infinitely original."[13]

- "God created man in his own image, in the image of God he created him; male and female he created them" (Genesis 1:27).

Thought 2: The product of God's imaginary thoughts were good and perfect.

- "God looked over everything he had made; it was so good, so very good!" (Genesis 1:31, MSG).
- "Everything God created is good" (1 Timothy 4:4, NIV).

Thought 3: The product of God's imaginary thoughts was freedom.

- "The LORD God commanded the man, saying, 'You may surely eat of every tree of the garden, but of the tree of the knowledge of good and evil you shall not eat, for in the day that you eat of it you shall surely die'" (Genesis 2:16-17).

Thought 4: The product of God's imaginary thoughts was man and woman perfect but needy.

- "The LORD God said, 'It is not good that the man should be alone; I will make him a helper fit for him'" (Genesis 2:18).

Thought 5: The product of God's imaginary thoughts was a portrait of peace and harmony.

- "The serpent was clever, more clever than any wild animal GOD had made. He spoke to the Woman" (Genesis 3:1, MSG).
- The idea here is that there was no conflict between God's creation because sin had not yet entered the world, therefore there was no need for Eve to be alarmed that a snake was speaking her. Before the Fall, fear was not yet an emotion that humans experienced.

Thought 6: The product of God's imaginary thoughts was a perfect relationship with man and woman.

- "They heard the sound of the LORD God walking in the garden in the cool of the day" (Genesis 3:8).

In creation we see the product of the infinitely original and innovative God imagining and crafting the heavens and the earth. What God made was perfect and good, and from this plot movement we are afforded a backstage pass to God's imaginary thoughts. The ability to imagine is part of what it means to be created in the image of God. We are a product of his imaginative energy, and since we are like God, we too have imaginative energy. So from creation we know that God has given the ability to imagine and create. This is further demonstrated in that Adam was given the responsibility to invent names "to all livestock and to the birds of the heavens and to every beast of the field" (Genesis 2:20). Therefore, the ability to use imagination existed prior to the Fall.

PLOT MOVEMENT 2: OBSERVATIONS FROM THE FALL

Thought 1: The gift of imagination was used to rebel against God.

- "Did God actually say . . . ?" (Genesis 3:1).
- "The serpent said to the woman, 'You will not surely die. For God knows that when you eat of it your eyes will be opened, and you will be like God, knowing good and evil'" (Genesis 3:4-5).
- Notice how the Enemy painted a picture that required Eve to use her imagination in order to conceive the idea of rebelling against God.

Thought 2: The Fall affected all of mankind, including the imaginative ability.

- "Just as sin came into the world through one man, and death through sin, and so death spread to all men because all sinned" (Romans 5:12).

Thought 3: A depraved imagination has an inward focus that facilitates prideful thoughts.

- C. S. Lewis said, "Well, now, we have come to the centre. According to Christian teachers, the essential vice, the utmost evil, is Pride. Unchastity, anger, greed, drunkenness, and all that, are mere fleabites in comparison: it was through Pride that the devil became the devil: Pride leads to every other vice: it is the complete anti-God state of mind. . . . Pride gets no pleasure out of having something, only out of having more of it than the next man. . . . Pride always means enmity—it *is* enmity. And not only between man and man, but enmity to God. . . . For Pride is spiritual cancer: it eats up the very possibility of love, or contentment, or even common sense."[14]

Thought 4: A depraved imagination will reimagine decisions, activities, and circumstances by enabling a victim mentality.

- "The Man said, 'The Woman you gave me as a companion, she gave me fruit from the tree, and, yes, I ate it.' GOD said to the Woman, 'What is this that you've done?' 'The serpent seduced me,' she said, 'and I ate'" (Genesis 3:12-13, MSG).

If the first plot movement was a portrait of what the world looks like when God gets his way, then the second is a portrait of imagination gone wrong. Let it be understood that God did not desire for Adam and Eve and all mankind to fall into sin. Imagination was a gift from God; it afforded man the ability to be creative within God's creation. Sin was the mismanagement of that gift toward self-centered, prideful, and all-around wicked purposes. The presence of evil throughout history has always provided men's imaginations the opportunity to wander in a sinful direction. Had the story of our fall into sin ended with only the consequences of our insurgence, the word *hope* would have no place in our vocabulary—but immediately following our rebellion is the promise of Jesus (Genesis 3:15). In short, the "story of us" doesn't end with our demise. It has two more plot movements: God's redemption and restoration.

PLOT MOVEMENT 3: OBSERVATIONS FROM REDEMPTION

Thought 1: Redemption offers hope in the face of certain death, a new life that can be imagined. Redemption leads to hope; hope leads to life reimagined.

- The promise of death: "You may surely eat of every tree of the garden, but of the tree of the knowledge of good and evil you shall not eat, for in the day that you eat of it you shall surely die" (Genesis 2:16-17).
- The promise of life: "I will put enmity between you [the serpent] and the woman, and between your offspring and her offspring; he shall bruise your head, and you shall bruise his heel" (Genesis 3:15).

Thought 2: Redemption allows us to imagine a life that is fully human.

- To understand what it is to be fully human, we should study Adam and Eve before the Fall. They were in perfect relationship with God, each other, and the world that had been made for them. Therefore, to be reconciled with God is, in one sense, to become a pilgrim on a journey back to that perfect relationship. The end destination is the new heaven and the new earth; the journey to get there is redemption. Therefore, redemption allows us to imagine what it means to be fully what the One who created us intended.

Thought 3: Redemption allows us to imagine a different relationship with the cosmos.

- Bruce Ashford said, "The redemptive work of Christ extends through God's people to God's *cosmos* that in the end 'creation itself will be set free from its bondage to corruption and obtain the freedom of the glory of the children of God' (Rom. 8:21). The good end of God's redemptive purpose is a world in which the new heavens and new earth are formed, a world 'in which righteousness dwells' (2 Pet. 3:13), thus restoring God's good order for this world."[15]

Thought 4: Redemption reverses our alienation from God, allowing us to reimagine our relationship with others and ourselves.

- "Remember that you were at that time separated from Christ, alienated from the commonwealth of Israel and strangers to the covenants of promise, having no hope and without God in the world. But now in Christ Jesus you who once were far off have been brought near by the blood of Christ. For he himself is our peace, who has made us both one and has broken down in his flesh the dividing wall of hostility" (Ephesians 2:12-14).

The third plot movement shows us how God begins to move the world toward his desired ends. It is not yet a portrait of perfection and harmony as was seen in Creation, but with the new covenant (Jesus), the trajectory of human history has been redirected. There is now confidence among humans that God will get his way once again—because of the blood of Christ.

This is not to say Christ's work on the cross was not complete. Salvation is finished because his sacrifice was sufficient. It is simply to say that, while God's Son has been sacrificed, there is still more of the story to be told. When Jesus cried out from the cross, "It is finished," he was referring to his sacrificial work that made a way for our salvation experience. He was not, however, saying that this was the last act of the play. Redemption, as the third plot movement, makes way for the conclusion of God's grand narrative. The redeemed now see themselves as pilgrims progressing from this world to that which is to come.[16] As a pilgrim on a journey we think differently because we are heading to the Celestial City. We thus make decisions in the present in light of where our journey will end. Our thoughts and, for this discussion, *imaginations* have now been redeemed by Christ's sacrifice. This is why we call it a *redemptive imagination*.

PLOT MOVEMENT 4: OBSERVATIONS FROM RESTORATION

Thought 1: "God's work of redemption will reach its goal in the end, as God saves for himself a people and restores his good creation."[17]

- "This gospel of the kingdom will be proclaimed throughout the whole world as a testimony to all nations, and then the end will come" (Matthew 24:14).

Thought 2: Death is a curse and not a natural part of God's original plan, and thus it limits our imaginations; but even though our redemptive imagination is limited, it can have eternal significance. Our imaginings about real things should point people to the Redeemer.

- "The sons of the kingdom will be thrown into the outer darkness. In that place there will be weeping and gnashing of teeth" (Matthew 8:12).

Thought 3: Restoration points to the day in which God will ultimately get his way. As a result, our imaginings should be motivated toward that end, leading others to experience a little bit of heaven while on earth.

- "I saw the holy city, new Jerusalem, coming down out of heaven from God, prepared as a bride adorned for her husband. And I heard a loud voice from the throne saying, 'Behold, the dwelling place of God is with man. He will dwell with them, and they will be his people, and God himself will be with them as their God. He will wipe away every tear from their eyes, and death shall be no more, neither shall there be mourning, nor crying, nor pain anymore, for the former things have passed away.' And he who was seated on the throne said, 'Behold, I am making all things new'" (Revelation 21:2-5).

In the end, God gets his way when man's relationship to God is finalized — when those from all tribes, tongues, peoples, and nations become worshippers of Jesus and God fulfills his promise of a new heaven and a new earth (Isaiah 65:17; 2 Peter 3:13; Revelation 21). With this fourth plot movement, the story comes full circle as God restores what mankind and his sin had for so long torn down. We, meaning every human who ever lived, uncreated what God had so magnificently created.

Now couple the four plot movements of Scripture with these ideas:

- Because we are made in the image of God, meaning, among other things, we have the capacity to imagine . . .
- Then these four plot movements should inform our imaginations . . .
- Affording us the cognitive ability to recognize that things are not as they should be (think of every ill our society suffers from, such as disease, addiction, abuse, and so on), because we live in a fallen world . . .
- Leading us to ask the all-important question, What would it then look like if God got his way?
- And having the answer to that question motivated and guided by the biblical ideas of redemption and restoration.

In short, our imaginary thoughts about real things in this world should reflect God's desired will that is his grand narrative. This leads us to exercise a redemptive imagination; we will realize we are serving as ambassadors for Christ in this world.

ENGAGE

- How is theology practical?
- Describe the way the world looked when God got his way. What did it look like in the garden before the fall of man (plot movement 1)?

- Is the gift of imagination reserved for only a select few?
- The story God has told is the one true story that gives meaning to all other stories. Reflect on a recent story you have heard either through reading or going to the theater. Identify how the story echoes the four plot movements.

CHAPTER 2

THE RISE AND FALL OF CHRISTIAN IMAGINATION

Imagination is a womb that is impregnated with the old so that it might give birth to the new. It is the bridge that links the world around you with the world within you.

— WARREN WIERSBE, *PREACHING AND TEACHING WITH IMAGINATION*

Historically, the prophetic imagination has shown us that God's people are holy troublemakers, rabble-rousers and mischief-makers. We are folks who refuse to accept the world as it is and insist on moving it closer to what it should be.

— SHANE CLAIBORNE, PROMINENT CHRISTIAN ACTIVIST

The great instrument of moral good is the imagination.

— PERCY BYSSHE SHELLEY, ENGLISH POET

There is a kind of creative energy that once existed in the hearts and minds of the many dedicated to the Creator. They realized this creative energy or capacity is part of what made them fully human and citizens of earth and heaven. I have often wondered where it escaped. But maybe it didn't escape. Maybe, just maybe, it was left behind somewhere.

We have become a society of technology, believing all the while that technology is synonymous with creativity and imagination. Certainly technology is the *result* of innovation and imagination; many would argue that the mobile phone is one of the greatest inventions of our time. But could it be that while we have experienced innovation and ingenuity, we have simultaneously become hypnotized by the power of the digital age?

We need a level of awareness that can only be possible when we rise above the *Matrix*-like age we live in and scan the story line of history. More innovation and technology does *not* equal less confusion, fewer problems, less pain and suffering. So we can say with some confidence that we need to look beyond merely the products of the digital age. While products may assist in strategy and/or ideas for creative solutions, there is an undeniable need to look elsewhere.

We must discover something that was once lost: a type of imagination that can only be unlocked by those Christians who have experienced the redemption offered by Jesus. Thus, the best solutions can only be found by those who have been . . . well, found. With this in mind, let's explore some stories in which Christians used the gift of imagination to redemptively reimagine a better world. In each case, you will see reflected the plotline of God's grand narrative.

REDEFINE, REGAIN, REIMAGINE

Francis Schaeffer, a Christian philosopher and church leader who died in 1984, was a prolific and prophetic writer on Western thought and culture. One of his most popular books, *How Should We Then Live?*, opens with these words:

> There is a flow to history and culture. This flow is rooted and has its wellspring in the thoughts of people. People are unique in the inner life of the mind — what they are in their thought world determines how they act. This is true of their value systems and it is true of their creativity. It is true of their corporate actions, such as political decisions, and it is true of their personal lives. The results of their thought world flow through their fingers or from their tongues into the external world. This is true of Michelangelo's chisel, and it is true of a dictator's sword.[1]

The lack of a redemptive imagination and creative solution is a sad reflection on how little use people are making of their "thought world" for the glory of God. As we have already established, imagination is a gift and part of what it means to be human. To devalue or ignore this gift is to limit the potential impact one could make in one's family, culture, or church. The result of this cognitive complacency is that most people are bored. They find themselves in a state of boredom because they don't think for themselves; they just absorb the thoughts and worldviews from others around them. Schaeffer goes on, "Most people catch their presuppositions from their family and surrounding society the way a child catches the measles."[2]

To do such is to completely ignore the creative energy — wrapped in the gift of imagination — available to all. Yet every once in a while someone comes on the scene who challenges the system of thought and business as usual. Such individuals have been called a variety of names: heretic, visionary, insane, leader, quack, trailblazer, front-runner, martyr — and the list goes on.

No matter what they are called, they change things for the better. They refuse to stick their heads in the sand; they imagine a better way with a stubbornness that can only come from being right.

REDEMPTIVE IMAGINATION IN HISTORY

The process of redefining, regaining, and reimagining can be readily seen at strategic points throughout history. In the following events we will see examples of those courageous enough to recognize what was inconsistent with God's created order, and as such they redefined what had become. But recognition is only one of the three table legs to a redemptive imagination. In the events recounted below, different characters also used their voices and influence to cast the vision that something once lost must be regained. Finally, the courage to redefine and the declaration that something will be regained positions individuals throughout history to reimagine what could be.

When in Rome, don't do as the Romans.

In his book *How Christianity Changed the World*, Alvin J. Schmidt discussed the ancient Greco-Roman culture's view of human life, particularly as it pertained to infanticide, child abandonment, and abortion in the first four centuries of Christianity. Children were seen as objects and obstacles rather than gifts from God. They were discarded like we throw away an empty shampoo bottle. When was the last time you thought about an empty shampoo bottle after it was thrown away? This system of morality tossed children aside, never to think about them again.

The pagan practice of infanticide — killing newborn infants, usually soon after birth — was common in the Greco-Roman culture. Children were murdered for a variety of reasons. Some were killed because they were born physically weak or deformed. Other times families didn't want to have more than one daughter, so many females were murdered. Others were offered as sacrifices in pagan worship or simply killed out of convenience. While some were drowned, Schmidt notes others were more brutally killed, quoting the Greek historian Plutarch who says of the Carthaginians, they "offered up their own children, and those who had no children would buy little ones from poor people and cut their throats as if they were so many lambs or young birds; meanwhile the mother stood by without a tear or moan."[3] So common was the practice of infanticide that at least one early historian blamed the population decline of ancient Greece on it.[4]

If children were not directly murdered, oftentimes they were abandoned or aborted. It is hard for us to understand, but this was an assumed part of the everyday comings and goings of civilization at that time. There was no guilt or shame; Greco-Roman mythology even encouraged it. Schmidt tells us,

> The city of Rome, according to mythology, was reputedly founded by Romulus and Remus, two infant boys who had been tossed into the Tiber River in the eighth century B.C. They both survived and were reportedly reared by wolves. This mythology account is one of the many that reveal the Roman practice of abandoning undesired children.[5]

Abortion, as with child abandonment, was supported by even the most respected philosophers of the day, such as Plato, Aristotle, Celsus, and others. They demonstrated through their teachings and writings no reluctance to the practice of abortion.

Into a culture that murdered or tossed born and unborn children aside like empty shampoo bottles came Christians with their exalted view of human life. Under extreme persecution, the small movement of Christianity injected the Roman Empire with the cure for infanticide, abortion, and child abandonment—a doctrine of human life based on the teachings of the Bible. They believed humans were made in the image of God (Genesis 1:27). They believed the words of the psalmist: "You have made [man] a little lower than the heavenly beings and crowned him with glory and honor" (Psalm 8:5). They held firm to the teachings of Jesus about children:

> Then children were brought to him that he might lay his hands on them and pray. The disciples rebuked the people, but Jesus said, "Let the little children come to me and do not hinder them, for to such belongs the kingdom of heaven." And he laid his hands on them and went away. (Matthew 19:13-15)

This small group defied an empire—*redefining* what had become, *regaining* something that was once lost, and *reimagining* what could and should be. As Schmidt points out, Christians did much more than condemn infanticide, abortion, and child abandonment:

> They frequently took such human castaways into their homes and adopted them. Callistus of Rome gave refuge to abandoned children by placing them in Christian homes. Benignus of Dijon (late second century), who like his spiritual mentor Polycarp was martyred, provided protection and nourishment for abandoned children, some of

whom were deformed as a result of failed abortions. Afra of Augsburg (late third century) was a prostitute in her pagan life, but after her conversion to Christianity she developed a ministry to abandoned children of prisoners, thieves, smugglers, pirates, runaway slaves, and brigands. Christian writings are replete with examples of Christians adopting throw-away children.[6]

In the name of Christ, forbear!

Beginning a few hundred years prior to the birth of Christ, gladiator games were among the most popular form of entertainment in Rome. In our day, stadiums are filled to watch a sport that usually involves a scoreboard, athletes, and some form of equipment such as a ball or bat or shoulder pads. But for hundreds of years the Colosseum in Rome was filled to watch a "sport" of a different kind. Located at the center of the city, this amphitheater of death could hold over fifty thousand spectators who watched and cheered as gladiators systematically killed each other. These were usually people who were considered expendable: slaves, condemned criminals, or prisoners of war who had been put through training that further prepared them to fight.[7] Their equipment consisted of shields, swords, and armor designed to prolong and enhance the fight. The scoreboard could only be measured by the carnage and blood on the Colosseum floor.

During the fourth century, an Asiatic monk named Telemachus spent most of his days tending to his garden and fulfilling his vocation of study and prayer. But Telemachus felt the Lord leading him to go to Rome, the most wealthy and powerful city in the world. He didn't understand the purpose of the journey, yet he obeyed, making the long trip with everything he owned in a small bag he could throw over his back. When he arrived in Rome, the city was brimming with excitement and celebration over a recent military victory, and a central part of the celebration was the gladiatorial games. Telemachus followed the crowds as they filed into the Colosseum, where he took a seat high up looking down on the amphitheater floor. What he saw next both stunned and stirred him to action. He watched as gladiators took their positions and fought to the death. Each swing of the sword and the blood that followed caused the roar of the crowd to grow louder.

Telemachus immediately stood in his seat and cried, "In the name of Christ, forbear!" No one, of course, paid him any attention, so he began to walk down the stone steps and leapt onto the sandy floor of the arena. He promptly lifted his hands and screamed, "In the name of Christ, forbear!" At one point Telemachus fell to the floor due to a blow from the shield of one of the gladiators. It was an almost kind gesture meant to send the monk back to his seat. The crowd roared.

Refusing to stop, he rushed back into the midst of the fighting, shouting again, "In the name of Christ, forbear!" With a combination of laughter and cheers, the crowd shouted, "Run him through!" One of the gladiators lifted his sword and with one swift swing struck Telemachus, slashing him across his chest and stomach. As the little monk fell to his knees with his blood and guts spilling onto the Colosseum floor, he gasped and said once more, "In the name of Christ, forbear!"

As the monk's lifeless body fell, a strange thing happened: the crowd grew quiet. Then in the silence someone on the top row got out of his seat and left the Colosseum, then another, and another until the huge stadium was emptied of its spectators. Never again were gladiatorial games held in the Roman

Colosseum; never again was the blood of men spilled for spectators' entertainment. The courage and fortitude of one little monk had halted an entertainment industry created and sustained by the most powerful leaders in the known world — the Roman emperors.[8]

Telemachus redefined what had become of Roman society by pointing to the ungodliness of the gladiatorial games. He likewise helped a culture regain something that was once lost, some semblance of the sanctity of human life. Many times a redemptive imagination will begin with those who are willing to stand, alone if necessary, in the center of culture and say, "In the name of Christ, forbear!" Before we can reimagine what could be or verbalize that we must regain something that was once lost, we must have the courage and fortitude to redefine what has become.

Unless the divine power has raised you up . . .

John Wesley lived a very long time for a man of the eighteenth century. And what a life it was! "John Wesley averaged three sermons a day for fifty-four years preaching all-told more than 44,000 times. In doing this he traveled by horseback and carriage more than 200,000 miles, or about 5,000 miles a year."[9] The significance of his ministry can scarcely be understood. Hundreds of thousands must have been delivered under his preaching. More than 550 itinerant preachers and 1,500 local pastors, most of whom Wesley personally raised up, were influenced by this man's ministry.[10] His writing ministry includes a four-volume commentary on the whole Bible, a dictionary of the English language, a five-volume work on natural philosophy, a four-volume work on church history, histories of England and Rome, grammars on the Hebrew, Latin, Greek, French, and

English languages, three works on medicine, six volumes of church music, and seven volumes of sermons and controversial papers. He also edited a library of fifty volumes known as "The Christian Library."[11] Retirement was never an option; he continued to preach into his eighties. At age eighty-three he became frustrated with his own humanity in that he could not write more than fifteen hours a day without hurting his eyes. At age eighty-six, he again became faced with his own humanity, having to admit that he could only preach twice a day (but, astonishingly, in that year he preached in every shire in England and Wales).[12] John Wesley died in 1791 in his eighty-eighth year of life and his sixty-fifth year of ministry.[13] J. C. Ryle, a nineteenth-century Anglican bishop of Liverpool, said of Wesley's death, "He had always enjoyed wonderful health and never hardly knew what it was to feel weariness or pain till he was eighty-two. The weary wheels of life at length stood still, and he died of no disease but sheer old age."[14]

One of the more interesting aspects of John Wesley's life and influence is the last letter he ever penned. Ever since a missionary trip to Georgia early in his ministry, Wesley had stood against the evil institution known as the slave trade. He had written a treatise he called "Thoughts on Slavery" much earlier in his life, which many read but very few considered. He had stood against slavery his entire life but to very little avail. Therefore with his dying message—and the slave trade still in full swing—he reached out to a young man named William Wilberforce who had only been in parliament a few short years. This is a portion of that letter:

DEAR Sir,—Unless the divine power has raised you up to be *Athanasius contra mundum,* I see not how you can go though your glorious enterprise in opposing that execrable villainy, which is the scandal of religion, of England, and of human nature. Unless God has raised you up for this very thing, you will be worn out by the opposition of men and devils. But if God be for you, who can be against you? Are all of them together stronger than God? O be not weary of well doing! Go on, in the name of God and in power of His might, till even American slavery (the vilest that ever saw the sun) shall vanish away before it.[15]

In this letter, Wesley communicates first that unless one is called of God, one will not endure the task, and second, that slavery is a "scandal" of both religion and human nature. That is, slavery rejects the *imago dei* or humanity of those enslaved, treating them as animals or tools to be used and then discarded.

With his final act, Wesley *redefined what had become*, pointing out that slavery is inconsistent with Creation (plot movement 1) and a result of the Fall (plot movement 2). Wesley also attempted to *regain something that was once lost* through his writings, sermons, and influence (plot movement 3).

Unfortunately, this would not be accomplished in his lifetime. It is important to realize that *redefining*, *regaining*, and *reimagining* may take more than just one individual. In the case of the slave trade it took two lifetimes: enter one William Wilberforce.

One of the more interesting phrases in the letter is *Athanasius contra mundum*, which means "Athanasius against the world." Athanasius was one of the early bishops in the Christian church and had a reputation for courage and willingness to stand alone against heresy. With this reference, Wesley expressed to Wilberforce that if he took on this challenge, it would feel like he stood alone against the world.

But as history attests, Wilberforce did take on the world. Kevin Belmonte, a leading biographer of Wilberforce, wrote,

> His conversion to Christianity — his "great change" — had altered his destiny and, as events would prove, altered the destiny of Britain. Scarcely more than a year after his spiritual transformation, on Sunday, October 28, 1787, he found his life's work. On a blank page of his diary he wrote, "God Almighty has set before me *two great objects*, the suppression of the slave trade and the reformation of manners."[16]

Wilberforce spent his life engaged in many social justice causes, but none more important than the abolition of the slave trade and slavery itself.[17] He would spend his entire adult and professional life as a politician fighting the slave trade; in fact, the abolition of the slave trade in England would not take place until just days before his death.

Wesley *redefined* what was right and championed the cause of *regaining* a biblical sense of humanity for the slaves. And while Wilberforce would likewise serve in both roles, he would also *reimagine* a world without slavery. How would he employ a redemptive imagination and witness the restoration of slaves to their rightful status in society as human beings? Wilberforce employed imagination in a variety of ways:

- **In his relationships:** He listened to a variety of voices who all wanted to see the abolition of the slave trade.
- **In his calling:** He lived a life deeply committed to Christ in the public square.

- **In his strategy:** He employed various tactics with an eclectic group of people to move toward the abolition of the slave trade.

I encourage you to read a great biography (there are several to chose from) about William Wilberforce to find out more. My point here is simply to provide a bit of background and framework so that one can see how out of the ashes of the Fall arise those who will redefine what's at stake, regain what seemed lost, and reimagine things for the glory of God, as did Wesley and Wilberforce.

One More Example

History is replete with examples of those who employed a redemptive imagination to tackle some of the great injustices of their day—individuals like Elizabeth Fry, who lived during a time (1780–1845) when women held very few leadership positions in Europe, and yet her influence is still felt today. The social injustice she opposed during her life was the deplorable and brutal conditions of England's prisons in the early 1800s. Most at that time accepted the notion that the prison systems existed only for punishment, not reform. Additionally, most believed very little care should be given to the quality of life a prisoner experienced while incarcerated. Elizabeth Fry disagreed on both accounts and spent her life initiating a number of prison reforms that are still practiced today.[18] Biographer June Rose wrote, "Through her passionate crusade she succeeded in rousing the world's conscience to the pitiable state of women in prison and in creating a glimmer of sympathy for the lunatics and the poor."[19]

Mrs. Fry could have easily faded into the pages of history

had she done nothing to reform prison conditions. She could have blamed her low status in society on her sex and/or culture. She could have blamed the magnitude of the problem on the system that allowed such deplorable prison conditions for women. But those who reimagine for the glory of God really don't have time or the mind-set for excuses; their lives are filled to the brim with ideas and action. Elizabeth Fry demonstrated the courage to redefine prison conditions for women, the perseverance to regain what was humane, and the vision to reimagine for her society and the world a better approach: reform instead of mere punishment.

FLASHES OF GENIUS: HOPE OF REDISCOVERY

As a whole there exists a great and increasing need to reimagine for the glory of God. The world we live in is sick (as a result of the second plot movement), one in which there are 163 million orphans,[20] 1.39 million trapped in the sex trafficking industry,[21] 20 to 30 million modern-day slaves,[22] 10.9 million children under five who die every year of hunger,[23] untold numbers of Muslims who die every day without Christ . . . and the list continues. The world needs people who will work tirelessly to reflect the plot movements of Scripture and tell a new story—one in which God gets his way in the present and not just the future.

There are flashes of genius and hope of rediscovery all around us. I recently read of one such instance in an article by Shane Claiborne, interestingly titled "Imagine a New World."[24] In it he argues the world is in desperate need of imagination and that historically,

The prophetic imagination has shown us that God's people are holy troublemakers, rabble-rousers and mischief-makers. We are folks who refuse to accept the world as it is and insist on moving it closer to what it should be. It's time for a fresh imagination. It's time to reimagine the world. Thankfully, God is good at dealing with a world in crisis — He has had a lot of practice. And the human imagination flourishes when times get tough, because we are forced to innovate.[25]

Claiborne reflects the four plot movements, the three roles (redefine, regain, and reimagine), and subsequent results of action in this passage.

- Those who *redefine* what has become, operating with a this-ought-not-be mentality: Claiborne states, "We are folks who refuse to accept the world as it is."
- Others whose message is to *regain* something that was once lost by declaring, "this ought not be": "Prophetic imagination has shown us that God's people are holy troublemakers, rabble-rousers and mischief-makers."
- Finally, those who *reimagine* how this world could be by demonstrating, "this is how now we should live": "We are folks who . . . insist on moving it closer to what it should be. . . . It's time to reimagine the world."

He goes on to give a couple of examples of those who have reimagined the world. In Philadelphia there is a church that opened its buildings to homeless people to have a warm and safe place to sleep overnight. City government told the pastor they were not allowed to run a "shelter" because they didn't have the proper permits; they were also informed they would not be receiving any permits because the city didn't want a shelter in that location. After much prayer and consideration, the church decided they wouldn't be running a shelter anymore; instead they would have a revival service that lasted from eight o'clock every night until eight o'clock every morning. Each night there is singing, worship, and sharing, followed by a ten-hour period of silent prayer.[26]

My prayer is that these "flashes" will become catalysts for others to activate a redemptive imagination. We see how a redemptive imagination has impacted history, and if we look hard and long enough we can see flashes of it today. If, as Paul said in Romans 14:5, you are *fully convinced in your own mind*, then the question of God getting his way now becomes very personal. With that in mind, let's now evaluate the mind-set necessary for activating a redemptive imagination.

ENGAGE

- Identify another cultural crisis in history or present day (examples could be abortion or sex trafficking). How are people using a redemptive imagination to bring about God-honoring solutions? As you go through this process, identify the messages (redefine, regain, reimagine).
- What are some of God's desires that are not being met in the culture or community where you presently live? (Remember, a redemptive imagination can be the bridge between the desired will of God and obedience to the faith.)

CHAPTER 3

A NEW KIND OF NORMAL:

Activating a Redemptive Imagination

All of imagination — everything that we think, we feel, we sense — comes through the human brain. And once we create new patterns in this brain, once we shape the brain in a new way, it never returns to its original shape.

— JAY WALKER, CURATOR OF THE LIBRARY OF HUMAN IMAGINATION

As myth transcends thought, Incarnation transcends myth. The heart of Christianity is a myth which is also a fact. The old myth of the Dying God, without ceasing to be myth comes down from the heaven of legend and imagination to the earth of history. It happens — at a particular date, in a particular place, followed by definable historical consequences. We pass from a Balder or an Osiris, dying nobody knows when or where, to a historical Person crucified (it is all in order) under Pontius Pilate. By becoming fact it does not cease to be myth: that is the miracle.

— C. S. LEWIS, GOD IN THE DOCK

I should like to be able to believe that I am here in a very small way contributing . . . to the encouragement . . . of story that can mediate imaginative life to the masses while not being contemptible to the few.

— C. S. LEWIS, OF OTHER WORLDS: ESSAYS AND STORIES

God has told a story. Correction—God has told *the* story, as we have seen in chapter 1. It is a story that determines all others. No matter how hard a storyteller may try, no matter how dark or perverse a story may be, inevitably it can only be understood in light of God's story. The darkness and perversity can only be understood in light of the Fall. Any redemption that may or may not take place inevitably exists because *the* story has a redeemer. Likewise, any resolution, clarity in the end, or finality that a story may present is only offered because this mess of a world will be restored. Yes, God has told *the* story, and now as redeemed imagineers it is our privilege to tell another, one that reflects the creative plot movements of God's story. Our stories will inevitably reflect God's; this much is not up for debate. What should concern and ignite our imaginations is *how* we get to express or live our story.

Will our stories accentuate the positive of the Creation plot movement? This sounds like an intriguing and God-honoring endeavor but ignores the fact that we live in a fallen world with real-life consequences swirling all around us. A story that looks only on the bright side never solves any problems; the world is always one step removed from the storyteller. It should be understood that it doesn't take a lot of courage to retreat. On the other hand, some stories represent a rabbit hole of darkness void of any hope or light of day. These are the pessimistic storytellers who have a stifled imagination with a defeatist attitude toward culture.

I don't know which is worse. But those who focus only on the redemption plot movement don't have the entirety of the story either; they don't go far enough. They tend to think that the redemption plot movement erases the Fall. They fail to understand that a redeemer neither erases nor eradicates poverty, pain, tragedy, loneliness, sexual confusion, or any other human or social ill. No, Jesus won't necessarily make you rich, pain- or tragedy-free, popular, inclined toward a godly sexuality, and so on. Jesus didn't erase the Fall; he is not the Great Magician. Redemption does not make the consequences of a fallen world disappear; it simply points us toward restoration for the completion of the story. Redemption, the kind Jesus offers, makes a way out of the darkness into God's light. He calls us to himself, burdens and afflictions and all. So to focus only on the redemption plot movement really prohibits the storyteller from experiencing a story in which "Christ is all, and in all" (Colossians 3:11).

Just as it is incomplete to focus solely on any one of the first three plot movements—creation, fall, or redemption—it is impossible to focus only on the plot movement of restoration. Restoration can only be discussed in light of the three previous plot movements. Restoration recalls the perfect picture of Creation and the need for redemption because of the Fall.

So tell a story that adequately reflects God's, for it is then that *he* is most obvious in *our* story. We must tell a story, and by tell a story I mean *live* a story, that would make the Great Storyteller proud. Yes, it will be chock-full of drama, disappointment, unforeseen twists and turns, but it will begin at the feet of Jesus (creation) and thus end at the feet of Jesus (redemption changing the trajectory of things toward restoration). And we shouldn't buy into the notion that we are not storytellers or we are not creative. This is to deny the gift of imagination we have been given and to deny part of what it means to be created in the image of God. Everyone is creative because everyone has been created. And to that we sing, "Praise God, praise God, praise God."

Understanding that we all have been given a gift of imagination serves as a gateway to a new kind of normal, a new way of looking at our life. Our life is a story that we tell, and God allows us to tell it using a redemptive imagination. A *redemptive imagination* is creative thinking applied to real-life problems. It gives us (finite beings) the ability to explore infinite possibilities, if we have abandoned ourselves to Jesus. We were made for this, as has already been demonstrated, and this is part of what it means to be human. But as Warren Wiersbe said, "We have forgotten that the bridge between the mind and the will is the imagination, and that truth isn't really learned until it's internalized."[1]

In order to accomplish significant things, we must first be able to think about significant things. To tell a great story we must first imagine a great story. Remember, "For as [a man] thinks in his heart, so is he" (Proverbs 23:7, NKJV). Therefore, we reflect God's story by redemptively reimagining life.

PRACTICAL IMPLEMENTATION OF A REDEMPTIVE IMAGINATION

In one sense, we are retraining our brains how to think about life. For some this is a new model, a new kind of normal, which will fit hand-in-glove. For others it will be a difficult struggle for a variety of reasons. Some of us have thought a certain way for so long we have only one view of life. The idea of our life being a story that is a result of our imagination reflecting God's imagination is foreign and awkward.

We can implement habits to encourage a new way of thinking—the way of the redemptive imagination. Think of these habits as ways to embrace and navigate our imaginary thoughts about real things.

Pray: "Oh, God, awake my soul to solutions."

When seeking to reflect God's story in a way that honors him, it is important to begin with that most intimate of Christian activities: prayer. Because we "were created in the image of God, created by an imaginative God who is infinitely original," we were also "created to cultivate [our] inner person—including [our] imagination—and use all that [we] are to the glory of God."[2] At this point we see imagination as an incredibly powerful spiritual tool. Bible teacher W. Ian Thomas wrote, "Our spirituality is simply our availability to God for His divine activity."[3] So through prayer we are asking God to awaken our imaginations.

I once read that many of us view God as a divine bellhop, ever available to fulfill our requests. In this metaphor, prayer is the equivalent of sitting in a hotel room, picking up the phone, and asking room service to bring us a meal or pick up our laundry.[4] As someone who spends a great deal of time on the road and in hotel rooms, I was certainly convicted by the analogy. The convenience and luxury of picking up the phone to order a meal, get a wake-up call, or have someone pick up my laundry couldn't be how I had approached God through prayer, could it? Then I began to actually listen to the words of my prayers, and the results of this experiment took me completely by surprise. I began to pray out loud at the end of my quiet time and realized that my prayers had fallen into a predictable rut of saying the same thing over and over. I generally asked God to forgive me of my sins and asked him to bless me in certain ways. I'd ask him to bless others, again generally. What had happened to my prayers was both predictable and shameful. I had reduced God, in my mind, to divine room service. He existed for me, as opposed to the other way around.

E. Stanley Jones, an extraordinary Methodist missionary to India in the twentieth century, described prayer in his autobiography *A Song of Ascents*:

> Prayer is surrender — surrender to the will of God and cooperation with that will. If I throw out a boat hook from a boat and catch hold of the shore and pull, do I pull the shore to me, or do I pull myself to the shore? Prayer is not pulling God to my will, but the aligning of my will to the will of God.[5]

When we read these words, we should do so with the central question of this book in mind. What would it look like if God got his way? This allows us to view prayer as the opportunity to position ourselves with the will of God. We make ourselves available to him. I am convinced God fills our redemptive imaginations when we are receptive to his will.

Prayer is important to all who wish to serve God with their imaginary thoughts about real things. John Bunyan, the author of *Pilgrim's Progress*, said it this way: "You can do more than pray after you have prayed, but you cannot do more than pray until you have prayed."[6]

Marinate thinking in the Scriptures; the longer something marinates, typically, the better it tastes.

The goal of our imaginary thoughts is to make stories — life changes — that contain solutions based on truth. Therefore, the best imaginations are colored by a view of God as revealed in his Word. Warren Wiersbe wrote, "Blessed is that Bible student who comes to God's Word with an open mind, a loving heart, a submissive will, *and a sensitive imagination*."[7] If the Bible, the grand story God has told, defines reality, then our thoughts should take residence inside the Scriptures. There our thoughts are positioned to redefine what has become, regain what has been lost, and reimagine what could be. The more time we spend reflecting on the Scriptures, the greater is our capacity to imagine.

Experience special revelation in the context of general revelation.

Here's an idea to enhance creativity: Read the Bible outside in God's creation or go for a walk through a part of God's creation immediately after. The digital age keeps us inside far too much. But there is no substitute for venturing outside — not even a great screensaver of a mountain or tropical fish tank. Getting out into the sun daily contributes to our health and, in turn, to our creativity. There are consequences of overexposure to the sun, of course, but Dr. Robert S. Stern, chair of the department of dermatology at a Harvard-affiliated medical center, says we have gone too far with sun dread and become "solar-phobes."[8] He goes on to say,

> The same DNA-damaging, sunburn-causing UVB wavelengths that sun-screens are designed to block also do some good: They kick off the chemical and metabolic chain reaction that produces vitamin D. Research shows that many people have low vitamin D levels. There is a well-documented relationship between low vitamin D levels and poor bone health. . . . Getting some sun may also shake off the wintertime blues: Research suggests that light hitting your skin, not just your eyes, helps reverse seasonal affective disorder (SAD). Moreover, being outside gets us golfing, gardening, and engaging in other types of physical activity.[9]

In other words, vitamin D levels affect our health and our moods, which affect our ability to function well. This is important for our present conversation because a redemptive imagination is a new way to think—it requires more of us than we may be accustomed to.

Never believe the solution can't be found, but realize it may be beyond present ability.

This may seem like a depressing thought at first glance, but the fact is we may only be part of the solution (tell part of the story). Remember, John Wesley (chapter 2) never saw the abolition of the slave trade in his lifetime. If one were to consider Wesley's life only on that issue, his story would be without a happy ending. But to stop the story there would be foolish because when Wesley died, he "left the lights on": The story of the slave trade did not stop but rather had only begun. Wesley would only redefine; it would be left to others to regain and reimagine the rest.

See, the story we *tell* with our life will inevitably be bigger than our life. We may not be around for the ending, the final scene, or the credits. This is a good thing, since being there when the credits roll would probably lead to us taking credit. We serve God better thinking of ourselves as part of the cast, while he is the director. If that is, in fact, the mind-set, then success is found in telling a story that others will want to continue.

And remember, just because we cannot arrive at a solution in the present doesn't mean that one can't be discovered. It just means we aren't at that part of the story yet. The belief that solutions cannot be found is thoroughly pessimistic; it's the anti-God attitude. If the problem is real (the Fall), a real solution exists, waiting to be discovered and implemented (redemption and restoration).

The first, second, or one-hundred-seventieth try may not be the right solution.

If the fuel for imagination is grace — a theme at the center of God's story — the tank will never run dry. Therefore our imaginations must have a tenacious quality about them as we seek to change the world. One of the great examples of grace-fueled tenacity in Scripture is Abraham's conversation with God in Genesis 18:22-33 concerning the city of Sodom. Upon hearing the news that the sins of Sodom and Gomorrah were so great that God was going to destroy the city, Abraham stayed in the presence of God and argued with him:

> Abraham confronted [God], "Are you serious? Are you planning on getting rid of the good people right along with the bad? What if there are fifty decent people left in the city; will you lump the good with the bad and get rid of the lot? Wouldn't you spare the city for the sake of those fifty innocents? I can't believe you'd do that, kill off the good and the bad alike as if there were no difference between them. Doesn't the Judge of all the Earth judge with justice?"
>
> GOD said, "If I find fifty decent people in the city of Sodom, I'll spare the place just for them."
>
> Abraham came back, "Do I, a mere mortal made from a handful of dirt, dare open my mouth again to my Master? What if the fifty fall short by five — would you destroy the city because of those missing five?"
>
> He said, "I won't destroy it if there are forty-five."
>
> Abraham spoke up again, "What if you only find forty?"
>
> "Neither will I destroy it if for forty."

He said, "Master, don't be irritated with me, but what if only thirty are found?"

"No, I won't do it if I find thirty."

He pushed on, "I know I'm trying your patience, Master, but how about for twenty?"

"I won't destroy it for twenty."

He wouldn't quit, "Don't get angry, Master — this is the last time. What if you only come up with ten?"

"For the sake of only ten, I won't destroy the city."

When God finished talking with Abraham, he left. And Abraham went home. (MSG)

Notice first that Abraham stayed in the presence of God; he drew near to God. *The Message* says, "Abraham stood in God's path, blocking his way" (verse 22). He was determined to be heard. What followed was an expression of tenacious grace as he begged for the lives of the citizens in Sodom. The conversation is really one-sided, with Abraham doing most of the talking; yet the conversation reveals more about God's character than it does about Abraham's. There are two things worth noting in the passage about tenacity. First, Abraham expressed a series of six what-ifs. What if fifty? Forty-five? Forty? Thirty? Twenty? Ten? And second, God tolerated Abraham's petitions! What if God did more than tolerate? What if he delighted in his servant tenaciously pleading that the lives of citizens would be spared? I am convinced that if Abraham's grace-fueled tenacity were in any way wrong, then God would not have tolerated it. So let it be understood that our role is not to throw in the towel or wish for judgment. Judgment is not in our hands; the end of a story is in God's hands. Our role is to see it through, to come back to our spiritual drawing board—the Scriptures and prayer—in an effort to never stop telling the story until God says, "Well done."

Create a synergy of biblically based imaginary thoughts about real things.

One of my favorite classes in seminary was on the life and influence of C. S. Lewis, taught by Dr. Michael Travers. Much of what I know about Lewis originated from that class, and for it I am forever grateful. One of the more interesting aspects of Lewis's life was his particular relationship with Tolkien. While Tolkien had an impact on converting Lewis to Christianity, the two also impacted all of literature together. Unsatisfied with the quality of fiction being published, the men decided to remedy the situation with the following plan: Lewis would write about another world, and Tolkien would write about another time. Needless to say, it wasn't a bad team or plan. Throughout the writing process they would gather in a pub for the purposes of reading and critiquing each other's manuscripts. Now think about this for a moment—two of the greatest literary minds of the last hundred years believed it important to share the expression of their imaginations for the purposes of improving the story they sought to tell. What a synergy for creative thought! Who wouldn't have loved to be over in the corner of that pub listening to the conversations?

What a great example that Lewis and Tolkien set to show the benefit to the creative process by critiquing each other's ideas! Imaginary thoughts kept inside one person's head are essentially imprisoned with no hope of being released. A group in which the expression of imaginary thought is welcomed and encouraged is more than the sum of its parts. I am by no means suggesting we express these thoughts with just anyone willy-nilly, but with a person or group who cares deeply about reflecting God's story. The group doesn't even necessarily have to desire the same change as its individuals do, so long as it is engaging in the same process that produces the answer to the ultimate question: What would it look like if God got his way?

Thoroughly understand the problem so a solution can be thoroughly imagined.

If the best stories are the ones that reflect the four plot movements of God's story, it serves to reason we must seek to understand the problem. In other words, we must answer the how-we-got-here question, so as we imagine a solution we don't fall prey to previous mistakes.

To accomplish this we must be relational, willing to get close to the mess that needs to be fixed or the pain that needs to be addressed. Many times, actors will engross themselves in a character when preparing to play that part on a screen; if the actor is playing a homeless person, he or she may live as a homeless person to better understand the risks, emotions, and overall condition of being homeless. Likewise, if an American actor has an upcoming role in which he plays a character in the German army during World War II, that actor might study German culture from that time and attempt to perfect the German accent.

The redeemed who imagine, on the other hand, are not simply retelling someone else's story. We are telling our own story, and in so doing, reflecting and being a part of God's story. That is why we must understand the problem so that we can imagine a new way forward.

This doesn't mean that we must experience to understand. We don't always have to experience something to discover how beauty can replace ugliness. Wilberforce wasn't a slave, but he became a student of the slave trade so he could abolish it. He studied the condition of a slave traveling from his homeland during weeks at sea crammed into a ship like cargo; he observed being sold on the auction block and the inhumane work conditions. He became a student of the slave trade so he could imagine a world in which slavery did not exist.

It may get messy before it gets neat, and after it gets solved, it may still be messy.

Clarity is not synonymous with neatness. Reimagining what could be and reflecting the fourth plot movement (restoration) is not a gateway to a perfect world. There will still be messes even after the application of our imaginary thoughts. The reason for this is that we are telling a story by reflecting God's story. It is only when God fully restores that the entirety of the mess will be cleaned up. Until then we must operate within the reality that fallen people are involved and will thus impact the product of our redemptive imaginations. There will be drama, confusion, pride, insecurities, and a host of other by-products of depraved humanity surrounding hard-fought solutions the Lord has allowed us to envision. After we recognize, regain, and reimagine, there will be those who don't understand how we arrived at the solution or even agree with it. And here is the real kicker: Even after we have reimagined, it may get broken again. So get semicomfortable with the mess — and at the same time never accept it.

ENGAGE

- What is the danger of focusing on only one plot movement, as opposed to considering the entirety of the story? How can a narrow focus inhibit one from redefining, regaining, and reimagining?
- The redemptive imagination process is, in many ways, a different kind of approach. What are some mental disciplines or convictions that will help prepare you to experience a redemptive imagination?
- Identify two or three of the above-mentioned disciplines and then think about how they can be implemented in your life.

CHAPTER 4

DREAMING WITH THE LIGHTS ON:
Applying a Redemptive Imagination

All men dream, but not equally. Those who dream by night in the dusty recesses of their minds wake in the day to find that it was vanity: but the dreamers of the day are dangerous men, for they may act their dream with open eyes, to make it possible.

— T. E. LAWRENCE, BRITISH ARMY OFFICER WHO BECAME KNOWN AS LAWRENCE OF ARABIA

The Storyteller's Creed:
I believe that imagination is stronger than knowledge.
That myth is more potent than history.
That dreams are more powerful than facts.
That hope always triumphs over experience.
That laughter is the only cure for grief.
And I believe that love is stronger than death.

— ROBERT FULGHUM, ALL I REALLY NEED TO KNOW I LEARNED IN KINDERGARTEN

Invitation:
If you are a dreamer, come in . . .
For we have some flax-golden tales to spin.

— SHEL SILVERSTEIN, WHERE THE SIDEWALK ENDS

In one sense what we are discussing can be explained as a vision for life, or maybe a more adequate term would be a dream. The world is in need of those who would dare to employ a redemptive imagination and dream about what could, should, and will happen as a result of their dreams. *Where have all the dreamers gone?* is a great question but not one that is too difficult to answer. As we've established, imagination, and thus a "conscious dream," is part of what it means to be human. So where have all the dreamers—and the potential power of their imaginations—gone?

For many, imagination has gone dormant and is suppressed under the white noise of thousands of 140-character messages, more "friends" than we can ever possibly be friends with, online videos, and everything else that comes with a social media–driven society. If we're honest, we would have to admit that we have been lulled asleep, or at least hypnotized. It seems there isn't an ounce of our day not filled with messages, messaging, and the monotony of it all. Just yesterday we could unplug and be set free from the matrix of technology and the Web. Now, wireless capability means there is no escape. That is, unless we long for something more, something more human than online connections. If we do, we have the stuff dreamers are made of.

Anyone can have a lights-off, middle-of-the-night, unconscious dream. These are passive and can be explained scientifically. The dream that results from using a redemptive imagination, though, is better explained from a supernatural and spiritual perspective, as it is the active pursuit of what can be imagined while living one's life at the feet of Jesus.

GOD CAN USE US NOW

There is something liberating about the sacredness of *this day*. The active pursuit of a dream today, whether that means the discovery of the dream itself or the accomplishing of goals within that dream, makes the journey feel like a race and a daring adventure. Imagine for a moment fighting a giant or rebuking a nation at the age of seventeen, leading a country at the age of sixteen, becoming a slave at fourteen, assuming the role of queen at fifteen, or giving birth to an important child at thirteen. Sounds like something from the imagination of C. S. Lewis or J. R. R. Tolkien, not reality. You may think that, but you would be wrong, because these are all characters within the story that God has told.

- David was seventeen when he killed Goliath and between ten and twelve when he was anointed king.
- Josiah was sixteen years old when he took over the spiritual leadership of Judah.
- When Jeremiah was seventeen years old, God called him to rebuke a nation.
- Daniel was between twelve and fourteen years old when taken captive.
- Esther was fourteen or fifteen years old when she became queen.
- Mary was thirteen or fourteen years old when she gave birth to Jesus.
- James and John were both less than eighteen when called to follow Jesus.
- Timothy was fifteen to seventeen years old when he first met Paul.

There is one common theme among these teenagers: They believed that God could use them in the present. They believed *today matters and God can use me* now.

In his book *Today Matters*, John C. Maxwell articulates twelve key practices to begin thinking in terms of now:

Just for today . . . I will choose and display the right attitudes.

Just for today . . . I will determine and act on important priorities.

Just for today . . . I will know and follow healthy guidelines.

Just for today . . . I will communicate with and care for my family.

Just for today . . . I will practice and develop good thinking.

Just for today . . . I will make and keep proper commitments.

Just for today . . . I will earn and properly manage finances.

Just for today . . . I will deepen and live out my faith.

Just for today . . . I will initiate and invest in solid relationships.

Just for today . . . I will plan for and model generosity.

Just for today . . . I will embrace and practice good values.

Just for today . . . I will seek and experience improvements.

Just for today . . . I will act on these decisions and practice these disciplines, and

Then one day . . . I will see the compounding results of a day lived well.[1]

In each day, much could and should take place at a disciplined pace. That is the importance of lists such as this one. These daily applications afford us the ability to maximize each day's potential. A dream does not come to fruition overnight. It would be more helpful to think of redemptive imagination as a journey in which *today matters* and progress is made with a *God-can-use-me-now* mentality. According to Maxwell, there is significant potential in each day when the right practices are in place.

A DREAM HAS NO LIMITATIONS

What is a dream? When we take Jesus at his word, we know there are no limitations to what we can dream for the world. A redemptive imagination allows a dreamer to continually ask, "In the name of Jesus, just imagine if . . ." The dreamer wrestles with big questions — in light of the big story God has told — such as,

- What would I do if I knew I would not fail? or
- What would I do if every job in the world paid the same?

A dream involves embarking on a journey armed with the right convictions and willingness to discover what others haven't. In his book *Culture Jam: The Uncooling of America*, Kalle Lasn said, "'Dreams' by definition are supposed to be unique and imaginative. Yet the bulk of our population is dreaming the same dream. It's a dream of wealth, power, fame, plenty of sex and exciting recreational opportunities."[2]

Two Scripture verses are foundational to storyboarding without limitations. The first is, "Now to him who is able to do far more abundantly than all that we ask or think, according to the power at work within us, to him be glory in the church and in Christ Jesus throughout all generations, forever and ever. Amen" (Ephesians 3:20-21). What is so fascinating about this text is the emphasis on God's ability to answer prayer and our ability to ask and think. First, God is *able* from the Greek term *dúnamai*, which speaks of God's infinite capabilities. In short, there is nothing God cannot do consistent with his character. I say consistent with his character because God cannot, for example, lie, as that would be inconsistent with Jesus' statement *I am the way, I am the truth*, and so on. But it is safe to say that God's ability is not bound, and the text emphasizes this point by adding the double compound words *more* or *exceedingly abundantly*.

Finite man's prayers or potential thoughts will not limit God's infinite capacity. God is able to do superabundantly more than we even think.[3] The term *think* carries a wider range than *ask*, which is of significant importance to our discussion on imagination and creativity. You see, our prayers and even our potential thoughts will never exceed God's ability. Look at the way *The Message* supports this interpretation, mentioning both imaginary thoughts and dreams in this same passage:

> God can do anything, you know—far more than you could ever imagine or guess or request in your wildest dreams! He does it not by pushing us around but by working within us, his Spirit deeply and gently within us.
>
> Glory to God in the church!
> Glory to God in the Messiah, in Jesus!
> Glory down all the generations!
> Glory through all millennia! Oh, yes!

The second verse is, "I can do all things through Christ who strengthens me" (Philippians 4:13, NKJV). While Ephesians 3:20-21 focuses on God's ability, man's prayers, and potential thoughts, this text focuses on how the indwelling of Christ strengthens us for our tasks. If the fruit of your redemptive imagination honors and pleases God, he will strengthen you for every task necessary to see that dream accomplished.

Needless to say, this verse has often been misunderstood because the interpretation has been assumed. Paul wasn't making a comprehensive statement about the spiritual abilities of a Christian or saying that there is no limit to what a Christian can do.[4] What Paul is emphasizing is how we can be strengthened to do the will of God. Theologian Richard R. Melick Jr., commentating on this verse, wrote, "The will of God limited the application of the strength he knew. Many who misapply this verse step out of God's will for their lives. They hope to cover their actions by a blanket promise of power, but power comes in the will of God."[5] Think about this in light of our original question, What would it look like if God got his way? If your dream, the product of your redemptive imagination, is the will of God, the indwelling of Christ will strengthen you to see it come to fruition.

THE CHARACTERISTICS OF A DREAMER

There are six characteristics common to dreamers who seek to reflect God's story in how they use their imaginations.

The dreamer lets his or her view of God determine the size of his or her dream.

My wife is the mother to our children; this was and is her dream. Cultural influences did not determine this would be her dream; rather, it was her view of God shaped by a personal relationship with Jesus, study of the Scriptures, and the experience of godly parents. She is also a pretty well educated and talented woman! She graduated from an Ivy League college while working a part-time job at MIT. We attended graduate school together, where she proceeded to get better grades than I, even in theology classes, which stings a little. Following her graduate studies, she was offered jobs, had job interviews with great companies, and essentially could have pursued a number of vocational routes.

Then one day she walked in and announced, "I'm pregnant!" I would hear that same announcement two more times over the coming few years, and today, and every day, she lives her dream of motherhood. It means less income, older vehicles, and shopping at those big-box stores that sell everything in bulk, but we wouldn't even begin to call that sacrifice.

The dreamer begins by valuing that which matters to God. With *what God cares about* as the starting point, everything else takes form. Additionally, when the dreamer is so fixated on the dream, any sacrifices that need to be made along the way are almost unnoticeable. If it matters to God and sparks the redemptive imagination journey that results in a dream, sacrifice is like a gnat that may swirl around your face from time to time. You swat at it but never pay it any attention.

I realize my wife's example may seem like a small dream compared to eradicating disease in a country or bullying in a school, but if that's what you think, I would suggest your starting point is a little off. You see, the size of the dream is determined by your view of God, and if it matters to him, then all dreams are on level ground at the feet of Jesus.

The dreamer is not afraid to fail.

History is filled with those who had a dream and were not afraid to fail. There are many examples, but here are just a few.

My friend and mentor Dr. Jay Strack had the real privilege of being with the family of Dr. Martin Luther King Jr. when many of his archives were opened for the first time in years. Jay soaked up every moment, realizing it was a once-in-a-lifetime experience. One of the highlights of the evening was when Coretta Scott King opened one of Dr. King's college report cards and said, "So this is obviously before he was 'Dr. King'!" To everyone's surprise, the lowest grade that semester was in communication. The professor had written across the comments section: "Martin, if you continue to use that flowery language, no one will ever listen to you." Imagine what would have happened if Dr. King had decided he would never be a communicator worth listening to?

Here are more examples: Billy Graham's girlfriend broke up with him in college because she wanted to marry someone who was going to have an international ministry. Michael Jordan was cut early on from his high school basketball team. Walt Disney had his original character, Oswald the Lucky Rabbit, taken from him because, even though he created the character, he did not legally own it. Theodor Seuss Geisel, better known as Dr. Seuss, had his first book, *And to Think That I Saw It on Mulberry Street*, turned down by twenty-seven publishers. Following all the rejection and apparent failure, he wanted to burn the manuscript and attempt a different vocation.

There are two realizations we must come to concerning failure and a redemptive imagination. First, to fail along the way doesn't mean that one's imaginary thoughts about real things are worthless or wrong. They may simply need to be refined, or better yet, seen and heard by different people. The application of a redemptive imagination is, in many ways, part of the evolutionary process of an idea. The idea may need to further evolve or mature; it may not yet be ready for implementation. Or the audience may not be ready to receive it. In either case, the dreamer must continue to challenge the process and, above all, just continue.

Second, failure is not sinful. If a dream is the fruit of a redemptive imagination, it values what God values and is attempting to reflect the grand narrative of Scripture. Therefore, attempts that honor this process, thus honoring God, are, in fact, obedience to the faith—even if they fail at first. Failure can actually move us closer toward success and deepen our relationship with God, which means that God-honoring failure is actually part of sanctification.

The dreamer believes "If it's to be, it's up to me."

I have had some great and wise voices in my life thus far, and none more so than my own dad and Dr. Jay Strack.

My father taught me that if God calls you to something, he is summoning you to exhaust yourself to that task. From the age of seventeen on, I grew up hearing him say something that just about drove me crazy: "A call to preach is a call to prepare." That statement was both annoying and anointed. For some time I relied on raw talent as an excuse to give only part of myself to any number of tasks. I could talk myself in and out of almost anything I set my mind to. I would not have called myself a living sacrifice.

In Romans 12:1, Paul wrote to the house churches in Rome, calling them to action. He had already written that the whole earth was guilty of sin (3:20); that they had been acquitted of their sin and accepted into the kingdom (5:1); and that there was "no condemnation . . . in Christ Jesus" (8:1). But the fourth section of this letter shows how one is to live in light of these realities: condemnation, justification, assurance. To begin this section, he told them, "by the mercies of God, to present your bodies as a living sacrifice, holy and acceptable to God, which is your spiritual worship."

So the question becomes, what does it mean to be a *living sacrifice*? At that time a sacrifice was typically an animal whose entire reason for existence was for the moment it would be placed on an altar and have its lifeblood drained. In essence, it lived to die. Therefore, the application of this phrase is that Christians are to live realizing that each moment could be the last. It is a call to be a capturer of the moments of life in an effort to exhaustively offer up all of one's existence for his glory. It is a call to give all of oneself.

The second wise counsel, from Dr. Strack, is to believe, "if it's to be, it's up to me." At first the statement caught me off guard because it seemed to take God out of the equation. Jay later explained to me that if God has given us a dream, he has also given us the responsibility to act on that dream. The point is to live a life free from excuse and compelled by vision. Our responsibility is simply to do all we can to make our dream a reality—and then we are to trust God to do all that he can do.

The dreamer is willing to stand alone.

At some point, usually in the early stages of the redemptive imagination/dream actualization process, the dreamer will stand alone. I once heard the great coach Tony Dungy say, "Stubbornness is a virtue, if you're right." The process of a redemptive imagination will inevitably lead to some deep-seated convictions in your life, and for these convictions one must stubbornly stand with both feet firmly on the ground. This doesn't always mean that one will be standing alone against the entire slave trade or in the arena between two gladiators with over fifty thousand onlookers. The arena where your dream exists may be a family, a school campus, a sports team, an orphanage, a mental institution, or a village on the other side of the globe. But the dreamer and his dream will not go unnoticed, because true vision always attracts reality and those who will want to be part of the solution, even though it may take considerable time. In short, before you can have a cohort, you must have convictions. Before you can stand apart, you must be willing to stand alone.

The dreamer operates within his or her talents.

Aristotle taught that where talent and the needs of the world cross, success will be found. It is important to understand how God has gifted us. What talent(s) have we been given? The discovery and cultivation of our gifts may very well be the catalyst to a redemptive imagination and dream.

At Student Leadership University, the organization I help lead, we have taught a session on dreaming to thousands of students over the years. What is interesting is that when students are asked to share their dreams, it usually starts this way: "I feel like the Lord has blessed me with [specified talent], so my dream is to [fruit of redemptive imagination]." Or: "The Lord has really given me a heart for [redefine what has become] and [recognize this ought not be], therefore I am going to use my [talents] to [regain what was once lost and to reimagine what could be]." It is astonishing that in almost every case, the dream collides with the already-existing talent.

The dreamer is gospel-centered in his or her imagination.

A great example of this comes from a very unusual and unlikely place. In the Middle Ages most people were illiterate. This made the priest's task of teaching the Word of God all the more challenging, since the average parishioner couldn't pick up a Bible for himself. So how could the Bible be taught, other than just through oral communication? By turning the actual church buildings into symbols of the Word, in which every stone bore witness to the testimony of Scripture. Dr. Justo L. González, who wrote a treatment of church history in *The Story Of Christianity*, said,

> Medieval churches had two purposes, one didactic and one cultic. Their didactic purpose responded to the needs of an age when books were scarce, and there were not many who could read them. Church buildings thus became the books of the illiterate, and an attempt was made to set forth in them the whole of biblical history, the lives of great saints and martyrs, the virtues and vices, the promise of heaven and the punishment of hell. Today it is difficult to read these architectural books. But those who worshipped in them knew their most minute details, in which their parents and grandparents had read for them stories and teaching that they in turn had learned from earlier generations.[6]

Today these cathedrals seem like relics, tourist stops, or a testimony to the elaborate and ornate nature of the Catholic Church. To some degree that may be true, but if we are not careful, we overlook one of the great products of gospel-centered imagination. Somewhere along the way, someone decided to use tapestries to tell stories, stained-glass windows to let the light of Jesus in, sculptures to provide visuals for the story being told. At this point in history, the church was both the product and source for imagination. And if we go back into the halls of history and look closely, we discover someone had a dream for part or all of it. Someone had a dream in which families could learn the Bible, fathers could retell the stories in Scripture, and the faith of one generation would be retold to another. Someone had a dream that reflected the grand narrative God has told.

ENGAGE

- If a godly dream is the fruit of a redemptive imagination, what are some examples of modern-day dreamers? What was their dream, and did it reflect the definition we have learned from the Scriptures? Did the dreamer exhibit the characteristics outlined in this chapter?
- Quite simply, the dreamer and his or her dream are intended to change, improve, or eradicate something in culture. Therefore, take some time, unplug, go for a walk, and meditate on this question: What would I do if I knew I would not fail? Then, in the name of Jesus, just imagine if!

PART II

REDEMPTIVE IMAGINATION AT WORK

CHAPTER 5

WHEN DADDY SANG

I remember childhood trips to my grandmother and grand-father's house. They were filled with adventures, stories, and magical memories. We went on hunts for fictitious characters and rode the underground subway and pretend it was some-thing else altogether. Much of my fascination with story and imagination has its genesis in trips to my grandparents' house. As a grown man with three kids of my own, I often find myself taking my children on those same adventures and telling many of the same stories, encouraging the growth and use of the imagination every day.

I recently visited my eighty-eight-year-old grandmother, whom I have affectionately referred to as *Nannie* since I was four. Her age and physical ailments have not hampered her mind or her imagination. During my recent trip, we sat in her Georgia mountain home and discussed family, the Bible, and, of course, the new book I was writing. When I told her the premise, she began telling me stories. And at some point in our conversation, she told me the story of distant relatives I had never met or even heard of.

Apparently, my grandmother and her sister, Hilda, were very close. Through the ups and downs of childhood, which included a stint in an orphanage, they never left each other's side. This would certainly explain why my grandmother essentially lived in the hospital while Hilda was slowly dying. Now she is left with stories to tell her thirty-four-year-old grandson. While I knew of her sister, I didn't know much else. So on this trip she told me about Hilda's husband, Captain William Clement Hunter. She handed me a newspaper—the *Houston Press*, from July 7, 1961—open to an article titled "The Ship Captain Who Missed His Boyhood."

At the time the article was written, Captain Hunter had been on the sea forty-four years; since 1918, he'd been in virtually every saltwater port in the world. His father and grandfather were sailors too. Throughout his career he delivered cargo of all kinds all over the world. He even found himself involved in wars and military conflicts, including World War II and Vietnam. In the article he states, "After the second war I swore I'd never let the navy catch me again. But the ship was taken over in 1950 to transport Marines to Korea. We were in on the first landing at Inchon in 1950 and on landings on the northeast coast near Iwon. In 1951 we evacuated some 5000 civilians from Inchon."[1] When asked if any of his ships had ever sunk, he recalled being torpedoed in the South Atlantic during the war. Captain Hunter lived an extraordinary life, whether carrying cargo, delivering marines, or rescuing civilians. He was a strong leader who spent almost three hundred days a year at sea. He had three sons and two daughters, and the roughly seventy days a year he was home are where the greatest part of his story is told.

For this part of the story my grandmother turned to a manila folder and pulled out a document titled "When Daddy Sang." It was written by his daughter, Nancy Hunter Harrell, and the best description I can provide is that it is a reflection on a life well lived. Now keep in mind that I had never met Captain Hunter or any of his family, yet as my grandmother read to me, I felt myself drawn into his story. Because that is what good stories accomplish. Upon entering them you sense that somehow you are experiencing the drama, the ups and downs, and the surprises along with the characters. What follows is a story told, with her permission of course, by my distant relative Nancy. And though I have never met her in person, I have met her through her story.

It seemed as if Daddy had been away for forever. Although it had only been a few months, in the life of a very young girl, a few months can be forever. But now, tonight, Daddy is coming home! He will bring presents for everyone; he will listen to all of us and he will want to know everything we have learned in school while he was gone. We will get to stay up late and listen to Daddy talk and tell stories. But, after all that, Daddy will come into the living room and sit in the armchair at the right of the piano and say to me, "Play something for me, something to sing to."

There were so many times that I waited for my Daddy to come home from oh so far away. Bremen, Pusan, Antwerp, Yokusaka. I think that Japan was my favorite. Nobody in the world says Jap-an the way that my Daddy does.

But those trips are over. This last wait has been the longest, hardest wait and I don't know when Daddy will be home. He is coming from further than ever before. This time he is coming home from no exotic port of call, no open sea, no free wind, but from a most frightening place. A state of confusion, frustration, pain and fear.

"Daddy had a stroke," my mother said. It came on like a hurricane.

Somewhere in me lay the assumption that Daddy would simply get well and come home. He always came home. It had not occurred to me that anything would be different than before, however, nothing would be simple for Daddy again.

But in this great loss, Daddy has found greater courage. After many months, Daddy has gone from bed to wheelchair to walker to cane. But songs, tales and laughter are still locked inside of him. They are trapped behind tears, effort, struggle, frustration, and to a degree, isolation.

Sometimes at night I dream about Daddy coming home from his trips. I can still hear his voice in my dreams, the lilt and upward roll of his British accent and even the chop in his voice when he says Jap-an. In dreams Daddy is home and I can hear him singing while he is working in the yard, painting the garage, or working on the pump down at the bay.

But then I wake up and I can't remember the sound of his voice. It doesn't seem so big a thing for God to do, to give Daddy back his speech. I don't understand so many things. But Mama seems to. There is never a time when she walks past Daddy in his chair that she doesn't stop, sit on the arm of it and say, "Clem, don't we have so much to be thankful for?" Then she pats his arm and Daddy says, "Uh-huh." It's always that way with Mama and Daddy.

Months go by and the family gathers together for dinner. Afterwards my sister-in-law Madeline and I are at the piano playing and singing hymns one after another. Daddy came in and stood nearby as I turned the page to the Battle Hymn of the Republic. I began to play and Madeline sang the verse. Then, as we sang the chorus, the most beautiful, booming, familiar voice sang every word perfectly, clearly, and just the way that I remembered. Afraid to stop for the fear of never hearing Daddy's voice again, I played it again, and again, and again. And daddy sang it every time just the same. We sang until we could no longer sing for crying. Then he took our hugs and shrugged and went back to the family room.

That night when I said my prayers it was hard to contain my emotion. I had heard my Daddy sing again.

I share this daughter's reflection on her father's life with you at this point for two reasons. First, because I hope the emotion of the story grips you in some relatable way. I hope you sense the longing of a little girl to see her father, the sadness surprised by the joy of hearing his voice, if even for a brief moment.

To experience the emotion of a story is essential to understanding its essence and message. The story God has told (creation–fall–redemption–restoration) is the story of every Christian. In the garden we were guilty of destroying a perfect relationship with God, and thus needed to be brought out of the imprisonment of our sin. But we will one day be restored to a forever-perfect relationship with God in the new heaven and earth.

The story of this world reaches both throughout the generations and across cultures, while at the same time is infinitely personal. And because it is personal, it is emotional, though not exclusively. I am not reducing Christianity to "feelings, nothing more than feelings." However, it cannot be understated that our conversion — being fallen and destroyed but part of God's story to redeem and restore — is deeply emotional. In *The Pursuit of God*, A. W. Tozer wrote, concerning the lack of emotion: "The whole transaction of religious conversions has been made mechanical and spiritless."[2] He goes on to explain the idea of longing after God:

> I want deliberately to encourage this mighty longing after God. The lack of it has brought us to our present low estate. The stiff and wooden quality about our religious lives is a result of our lack of holy desire. Complacency is a deadly foe of all spiritual growth. Acute desire must be present or there will be no manifestation of Christ to His people. He waits to be wanted. Too bad that with many of us He waits so long, so very long, in vain.[3]

Emotion is necessary to understanding any story. If your soul is not stirred to some extent over the grace of God and your own story, then your mind may have been converted, but your heart is still dead in sin. This does not mean you wear your emotions on your sleeve, wave a flag, or raise your hands in every worship service; the emotion of which I speak is the "mighty longing" about which Tozer wrote. It is deep and it is undeniable.

Therefore, if emotion is necessary to experiencing or engaging a story, it is essential to a redemptive imagination. In the above story we long with the daughter to hear Daddy sing again. We don't want her to stop playing, we don't want him to stop singing, and we don't want this moment to come to an end.

But this leads me to the second reason for including "When Daddy Sang": the limitations of a redemptive imagination. A redemptive imagination reflects God's story in much the same way C. S. Lewis viewed myth and story as reflecting the one true story. But because it *reflects*, it is limited. The concept of myth was one of the major themes that wove throughout Lewis's career and conversion. In this excerpt from a letter dated October 18, 1931, Lewis explains his notion of myth:

> The story of Christ is simply a true myth: a myth working on us in the same way as the others, but with this tremendous difference that *it really happened*: and one must be content to accept it in the same way, remembering that it is God's myth where the others are men's myth: i.e. the Pagan stories are God expressing Himself through the minds of poets, using such images as He found there, while Christianity is God expressing Himself through what we call "real things." Therefore it is *true*, not in the sense of being a "description" of God (that no finite mind could take in) but in the sense of being the way in which God chooses to (or can) appear to our faculties.[4]

A redemptive imagination is limited for two reasons. First, because it can only reflect the one true story and in so doing, be part of that story. That is the mystery you must accept. And second, because it may only be able to provide a preview of what happens when God fully restores. It is limited in that it points to the one true story and it only offers hope by showing the hope that is to be found in God's story.

Captain Hunter's family, and in particular his daughter, wanted to hear him sing once again — and his song interrupted the present reality of someone living with the conditions of having had a stroke. But it did much more than that: Daddy's song was a preview of the coming attractions when God would fully restore him and he would forever sing again. In the same sense, the outcome of a redemptive imagination may simply be hope fueled by a mighty longing to one day see God and be fully restored. It is a hope that reminds us this is *not* as good as it gets and the story is far from over. It is a hope that is certainly enough, because when one knows with holy certainty where the story will conclude, the peace of God becomes your traveling companion.

- Why does emotion play such a significant role in experiencing and understanding a story?
- What are the limitations of a redemptive imagination? Why do those limitations exist?

In the following chapters you will walk the halls of a mental institution, stand underneath the Friday-night lights of high school football in Texas, meet a ministry that believes it can face a nation ravaged with AIDS, and much more. Some of the stories are simply a retelling of what actually happened; some are fiction loosely based on personal experience; others are a compilation of many already existing stories. But in each narrative you will experience a redemptive imagination at work or the consequences of the absence of a redemptive imagination. In some stories it is quite obvious, while in others it takes a bit more reflection to see. At the end of each story are explanations and a series of questions to help you engage the process of redemptive imagination. My desire is that by the end of this book you would have practiced and, through your own imaginative ability, experienced the stories — thus making the process less foreign to your thinking. So read on with the expectation that these stories are case studies to prepare us to answer the question, *What would it look like if God got his way?*

CHAPTER 6

CREATIVITY AND A DIFFERENT KIND OF CRAZY

I had no idea what to expect. After all, I had never been to a mental institution. I took out my wallet and left it under the passenger's seat just as a precaution. The outside building was nothing more than brick and concrete that had seen better days. I wondered as I entered the doors if that represented the types of people inside, people whose lives had seen better days.

Opening the door, I could hear, in the distance, a combination of screaming, yelling, and moaning. A very sweet lady named Jennifer greeted me and offered a tour of the facilities. She was not at all what I expected either. She appeared in bright, casual clothes — I think shorts and a T-shirt — and seemed to bounce through the institution; somehow I'd expected a slow, painful pace. Jennifer was actually excited to introduce me to her friends and tell me each of their stories. She was a special-education teacher employed by one of the local schools. Working at the mental hospital was her second job, and she did it for free. When I asked her why she served the hospital every week as an unpaid employee, she simply responded in a sweet country accent I had grown up with, "Well, my heart just breaks for these folks. Everyone else is scared and doesn't know what to do with them. But each of them has a story and the same needs as those who aren't institutionalized."

Jennifer never told me what exactly was wrong with each patient until after we had left his or her room. In their presence, whether or not they noticed or responded to her voice, she carried on a conversation dripping with compliments. She introduced me, the visitor, to each one.

We walked into the room of an older lady who was holding a baby doll and seemed to be staring off into the distance. The state had found her at the age of twelve, pregnant and living in a chicken house. It was thought the deplorable and inhumane conditions probably contributed to her illness. She would go on to have a normal baby, who would be placed in an orphanage and adopted. To this day she carries the doll as if it were her baby.

But not all the stories were sad through and through. One lady is only calm when she listens to country legend Kenny Rogers. Yep, that's right. So in her room, twenty-four hours a day, the bearded wonder sings. Another lady will take off all her clothes and walk around naked when no one is looking. Jennifer warned me that if I turned around and found a naked woman walking behind me down the hall, not to worry—it was perfectly normal. One middle-aged man's uncle had given him gasoline to drink when he was young. One young man in his twenties had been in a tragic car accident, and many others were simply born with some deficiency in their mental capacities. And death was a common but unwelcome occurrence.

My favorite was one patient who had possibly the greatest laugh I have ever heard — and if we got her going, she'd go on for minutes at a time. It was contagious, and after a minute, Jennifer, all the patients, and I were just laughing right along with her. Room after room contained unimaginable stories.

The state had made the decision to start the long process of shutting this institution down. Part of that process was to place some of Jennifer's patients in a group home, which meant they would not be given twenty-four-hour care. As she shared this with me, I felt I was standing in the presence of a dreamer who had the courage to believe *this ought not be* and who was further declaring *this shall not be.* She told me ten of her patients who had been moved to group homes in the last two years had died, and I sensed in the midst of her sadness a tenacity to redefine, regain, and reimagine another way until the last patient was taken from her care.

But the most shocking was yet to be revealed. Jennifer — not in an accusatory or frustrated tone — noted she'd received little to no interest from any of the churches in the area to be involved in the lives of these patients. She said, "I think they're scared of these people. They drive by the property every day on their way to jobs, going out to dinner, or taking the kids to soccer practice, and have just become accustomed to not thinking about this place."

I think that we need to redefine the term *crazy.* "Crazy" is driving by a mental institution filled with need and never imagining how God could get his way. Is God happy with the lonely crazies put in a corner, divorced from the lives of those who call themselves Christian? I would think not. What institutions could really use are a few more Jennifers who know the favorite soft drink of a particular patient (Mr. Pibb, not Dr Pepper) or who see the infinite value of someone who believes a baby doll is actually a baby. A redemptive imagination allows our story to merge with another's in such away that his or her story can be filled with optimism.

I know it may sound a little odd, but a mental institution can be a place where imaginary thoughts blossom into reality. In this setting, one is forced to tenaciously discover creative ways to relate to and befriend patients. But behind moldy bricks and concrete lies a sea of possibility. Down the halls of shiny hospital floors, cleaned with the kind of wax that reflects the fluorescent lighting above, are stories that could light up the world. Tucked away in dimly lit rooms are the obviously overlooked. The question is not one of opportunity but willingness—because open eyes will lead to broken hearts and motivated imaginations. I challenge you to walk the halls and meet the institutionalized to discover a story worth hearing and a story worth telling.

ENGAGE

Within thirty minutes of your home there is probably an institution much like the one I've described. Chances are that thousands of people drive by it every day and never stop to wonder about those inside. The broad phrases *mental disorder* or *disability* can be defined as "any clinically significant behavioral or psychological syndrome characterized by the presence of distressing symptoms, impairment of functioning, or significantly increased risk of suffering death, pain, or other disability."[1]

Throughout Jesus' ministry, he cared for and healed the disabled and afflicted: "So his fame spread throughout all Syria, and they brought him all the sick, those afflicted with various diseases and pains, those oppressed by demons, epileptics, and paralytics, and he healed them" (Matthew 4:24). Jesus valued these people. They mattered to him and thus should matter to his followers. They are disabled yet still infinitely valuable image bearers, meaning they can contribute to the church and the movement of Christianity. When Paul was describing the body of Christ in 1 Corinthians 12:22, he said, "The parts of the body that seem to be weaker are indispensable." Those who are more feeble or weaker certainly encompass those with mental disabilities, whether from birth or as a result of injury. Reformer John Calvin wrote that Paul "makes use of the term *weaker* here, to mean *despised*, as in another passage, when he says that he *glories in his infirmities* (2 Cor. 7:9)."[2] Think about that: Paul was telling us that those who would seemingly be despised are actually essential to the church. Those whom most would loathe should be loved by the body of Christ, and not out of guilt or some misguided obligation. We are to love them because they are part of us in the same way that the head and the heart are part of the same body. With that in mind, enter the process of redemptive imagination:

Redefine

- How are the mentally handicapped in the story despised? What about this story *ought not be*?

Regain

- What statement does Jennifer make by working for free at the mental institution? What, with her actions, is she declaring *shall not be*?

Reimagine

- What did Jennifer do to build relationships with those in the mental institution?
- How can someone with a mental disability be brought out of a place where he is despised (redeemed) and put into a place where he is indispensible (restored)? How can this be accomplished when someone is confined to a mental institution? How can this be accomplished when someone is not confined to an institution and able to participate when the church gathers?
- What would it look like if God got his way at the mental hospital?

CHAPTER 7

FRIDAY NIGHT AND THE LIGHT OF JESUS

Football in Texas is a religion. High school football, in particular, holds a special kind of allegiance and affection. Every fall, people file into stadiums where the Friday-night lights burn bright and everything else is put on hold. Attendees will endure rain, sleet, or snow before failing their team with an absence. And during the four quarters of live action, fans scream, cheer, and many times temporarily lose their minds out of some sense of duty. At the end of the night, little flickering lights on a scoreboard are all that matter. One team will lift its helmets in victorious celebration while the other bows in defeat. Likewise the corresponding sides of the stadium will either go quietly into the night or enjoy the spoils of victory. For fans and players alike, there is nothing like looking for a win on Friday night and feeling the high on Saturday morning after you have found one.

Yes sir, football in Texas is king. That is, until recently, when a head coach at a prominent school imagined a different kind of success . . . the kind that isn't found in flickering lights or one more *W* on the résumé. His name is Kris Hogan, and he serves as the head coach for Grapevine Faith Christian School. Grapevine is an affluent suburb of Dallas, with an athletic department made up of great coaches, the latest equipment, and involved parents. It boasts a healthy athletic program where both players and coaches strive to produce at maximum capacity.

What Coach Hogan did to shatter the traditional definition for success, ESPN columnist Rick Reilly called "the oddest game in high school football history."[1] The decision was to host the Gainesville Tornadoes, a team of players from a maximum-security juvenile facility with the most violent teen offenders in the state of Texas. Gainesville played every game on the road and typically had no fans at their games to cheer them on; after all, they were criminals. And while the label is true and unfortunately deserved, Coach Hogan believed they were much more than mere "criminals"; he believed they were infinitely valuable with the same needs as every other human being. One of those needs is to feel valued rather than ostracized, to be included rather than exiled.

Coach Hogan had the idea, *What if we prepared to serve them rather than to beat them?* He had played this team before. He'd seen what a game looked like from the field: an overflowing grandstand on one side, and on Gainesville's side, nothing. No fans, no support, and certainly no cheering. Hogan thought, *What if half of our fans cheer for the other team? What if a parent of a Faith player learns the name of a player from Gainesville and cheers for that boy?*

So he sent an e-mail to the Faith family, asking them to help support the Gainesville Tornadoes in the upcoming game. They did not disappoint. Some of those in attendance that night summed it up this way:

> Faith families formed a massive "spirit line" for the Gainesville Tornadoes players to run through. Parents held up a banner for the Tornadoes to burst through. Faith cheerleaders led cheers for Gainesville. Faith fans sat, en masse, on the Gainesville side of the field and rooted for the Tornadoes against their own children. They held up signs with the names of Tornadoes' players, and cheered for the boys all night long. The impact of that night was easy to see, from the expressions on the faces of the Tornadoes players, to the tears in the eyes of the Faith fans.[2]

Gainesville went on to lose 33-14, but on this night, the scoreboard did not decide success and the Friday-night lights didn't shine down on a stadium divided. You see, the love of Jesus made everything go topsy-turvy. The point of it all was not to score touchdowns and pad stats by playing an 0-9 Gainesville team; instead, it was to provide hope and communicate value. At the end of the game, the two teams assembled at the fifty-yard line for prayer, and everyone took his helmet in hand, bent a knee, and bowed his head. It was a fitting visual of what had been taking place all evening long, because that night was the product of a redemptive imagination.

Coach Hogan was heralded for the events of that night. Rick Reilly of ESPN wrote a column about the game; Coach Hogan was invited to attend the Super Bowl as the guest of NFL commissioner Roger Goodell and received the Sportsman of the Year Award presented by AT&T. A movie, called *One Heart*, is even being made based on the events of that night.[3] But Coach Hogan wasn't out to make a name for himself or his school. Rather, he wanted to make a statement to a group of young men known more for their mistakes than their accomplishments.

When asked by one of his players why they were doing this, he simply replied, "*Imagine* if you didn't have a home life. *Imagine* if everybody had pretty much given up on you. Now *imagine* what it would mean for hundreds of people to suddenly believe in you" (emphasis mine).[4] And that is just what they did; they imagined, in light of redemption, what could and should be that night.

For many in Texas, football is king and a religion, and every fall the Friday-night lights will continue to burn bright and the rest of the world be put on hold. But for at least one coach, Jesus is King and religion is caring for the obviously overlooked. Eugene Peterson renders it well:

> Anyone who sets himself up as "religious" by talking a good game is self-deceived. This kind of religion is hot air and only hot air. Real religion, the kind that passes muster before God the Father, is this: Reach out to the homeless and loveless in their plight, and guard against corruption from the godless world. (James 1:26-27, MSG)

On this night I believe Coach Hogan passed muster before God because he cared for those who were loveless in their plight. On this night God got his way as a coach and a school reflected God's story. While others have called it the oddest high school football game ever played, it could accurately be called Friday Night and the Light of Jesus.

ENGAGE

The obviously overlooked are all around, yet very few of us are willing to discover their stories. In the Creation account, God himself recognized that aloneness was not good and that his creation was not yet complete. In fact, before the second plot movement known as the Fall, God said, "It is not good that man should be alone; I will make him a helper comparable to him" (Genesis 2:18, NKJV). Dr. David Ferguson, who has championed the idea of a *relational theology*, interprets the verse this way:

> First, none of us can rightfully say, "All I need is God." To do so is to reject other people as a channel of God's loving provision. Adam lived in perfection with a deeply personal knowledge of God. If anyone had grounds to think his intimate relationship with the Creator was all he needed, Adam sure did. . . . The second implication is closely related to the first. Just as we cannot claim, "All I need is God," we cannot truthfully convey the message, "You only need God." To do so is to communicate a message of condemnation: "You should be able to take care of yourself without needing other people. If you still have needs, you don't have enough of Christ. If you were more consistent in your quiet time, if you had more faith, if you loved God with all your heart, soul, and mind, you would not be needy." As important and necessary as faith and quiet times and loving God are, God has chosen to involve people in meeting the needs of other people.[5]

With that in mind, I hope you see yourself as a channel of God's love and provision for someone who is lonely and overlooked. Their stories are known to God and are waiting to be noticed by someone who is willing to redemptively imagine a relationship.

Redefine

- How are delinquents in the above story living in a way inconsistent with God's creation? What about their stories *ought not be*?

Regain

- What was Coach Hogan seeking to *regain* by putting the Gainesville Tornadoes on the schedule? What was he declaring *shall not be*?

Reimagine

- How did Coach Hogan's attitude and actions reflect the four plot movements of Scripture?
- Imagine what it would feel like to be fifteen or sixteen years old and already an incarcerated criminal. What would it feel like to have no real family or friends recognize your value? What would it feel like to be "surprised by grace" and have an entire group of people communicate through word, deed, and relationship that you are valuable to them and infinitely valuable to God?
- Who are the lonely outcasts, the obviously overlooked in your community, and how can you creatively reach out to them and demonstrate their value to both to you and Jesus?

CHAPTER 8

FACE THE NATION

It was a Tuesday morning and I had just landed in Gaborone, Botswana, after a long two days of travel. The weather and country were beautiful, and I was excited about the task before me. For the next several days I would be privileged to teach at the School of Discipleship for a ministry called Face the Nation. This was my third year to be a part of this significant ministry.

I arrived at Open Baptist Church, where there was a roomful of college students from ten different countries. My assignment was to teach a biblical foundation for leadership, along with specified skills necessary for the leadership journey. It was a great opportunity to serve the kingdom, but if you were to venture just beneath the surface, you would see a ministry that is the product of a redemptive imagination.

Like many African countries, Botswana emerged from European rule in the 1960s. It was one of the poorest countries when it gained independence in 1966, but not long after, the discovery of diamonds gave Botswana one of Africa's most successful economies. Yet a booming economy is not all that Botswana is known for: It has the second-highest HIV/AIDS infection rate in the world (after nearby Swaziland). "Seventy-five people die of AIDS in Botswana every day, and every five hours another person is infected with HIV. More than 65,000 children have been left without parents because of the disease."[1] Roughly one quarter of the country's 1.6 million people are infected. Robert Guest, a respected author and journalist who covered Africa for seven years, wrote in his book *The Shackled Continent*,

> In several countries in southern and eastern Africa, a fifth or more of adults carry the virus. That does not mean that a fifth of the population of these countries will die of AIDS. It is worse than that. Almost all those who are now infected will die in the next ten years, but before they die they will infect others. In Botswana, the worst-hit nation, more than a third of adults carry the virus. The president of Botswana, Festus Mogae, lamented in 2001 that unless the epidemic was reversed, his country faced 'blank extinction.' He was not exaggerating.[2]

The entire situation could lead to a defeatist attitude. When government funding and programs that include education, billboards, and free protection have failed, one begins to understand why. When friends and loved ones die on a regular basis and children get passed from home to home, survival seems like the solution and eradication a myth that only the uninformed entertain.

Yet in uncertain times the redeemed who imagine refuse to accept what may appear to most a certain outcome. After all, we cannot forget the garden and how in the face of certain death, when there was seemingly no way out, God made a way with the promise of Jesus. In 2005, a pastor named Norman Schaefer, an elder named Akintayo Adedoyin, and the church they serve, Open Baptist Church, located in the capital city of Gaborone, decided to look for a way out. Their plan was strategic enough to be effective and simple enough to be understood by the masses:

> Our vision is to recruit and train available Christian students from the University of Botswana (U.B.) who go to the senior secondary schools as volunteers during the university's long winter break (May to August). These students have to be convinced about and live a lifestyle of sexual purity. They are to assist in the fight against HIV/AIDS through a program geared largely toward behavioral change and sexual purity (abstinence). They are deployed in schools in teams to teach life skills in the classrooms; help with sporting and other extra curricular activities; work closely with the Scripture Union (S.U.) groups in the schools; build relationships with the students and most importantly to live Christ on the school campuses.[3]

They have appropriately called this ministry Face the Nation, and throughout its young life it has had, at some point or another, an influence on every senior secondary school (our equivalent of high school) in the country. When Face the Nation began, no one had imagined a strategy that utilized Christian university students, no one had imagined accessing all the senior secondary schools in the country, and certainly no one had imagined the hundreds of thousands of dollars it would take to pull off this endeavor. But once the vision for it was in place, reality began to shortly follow. Modise Mokgwathise, the current director, compares the idea of Face the Nation to a little apple seed that was put into the ground. As the seed has grown into a tree, the "winds, cold, heat, pests, anxiously waiting for the rains, and working hard to keep the tree alive with the scarce water have all contributed to the excitement. But now we can see the beautiful blossoms and even the small fruits here and there."[4]

Face the Nation calls the university students, who go through training and serve, volunteers. Each year I am with these dedicated students, I cannot help but think of Jeremiah, who was also called to face his nation and did so faithfully. And just like Jeremiah, hundreds of volunteers respond to the call each year, willing and ready to face the nation. Some dynamic young leaders have emerged from this ministry.

I have personally observed a former child soldier go through the School of Discipleship and become a soldier of the cross. Many students rise above thousands of years of tribal traditions that involve ancestor worship to declare worship to the one true God. At present, there are students serving as missionaries to the countries that surround Botswana where they are starting their own version of Face the Nation. There are students serving in the public square and the private sector and the local church.

ENGAGE

Disease is the result of living in a fallen world. The Bible teaches that disease has four sources: God (Numbers 12; 2 Samuel 24:1,12-16; 2 Kings 5:27; 2 Kings 19:34-36; 1 Corinthians 10:8); Satan, though his capacity for harm is restricted (Job 1:12); sins of ancestors (Exodus 20:5; Leviticus 26:29; 1 Kings 17:18; Job 21:19; Lamentations 5:7); and the breaking of physical, mental/emotional, or moral laws of nature (Exodus 15:26; Proverbs 3:1-2).[5]

Before the Fall, disease did not exist. In other words, in the garden there was no AIDS, cancer, tuberculosis, polio, malaria, dementia, and so on. So while disease, in some cases, is God's punishment, the result of Satan's activity, the consequence of a previous generation, or simply the outcome of disobeying God's moral law, this in no way should lead Christians to apathy.

Instead, our attitude should be motivated and informed by Jesus. Remember that Jesus is the new covenant and, as such, takes a very different tone and approach to disease from the Old Testament. "He was nonjudgmental, interacting with them as people of worth, not as social outcasts. He was full of genuine compassion for them as suffering people — touching them, comforting them, healing them, and speaking normally and naturally with them."[6] In many cases, Jesus dealt with the spiritual issues first and then healed the disease. But it cannot be said he didn't care about a person's total health and wellness.

The modern-day disciple can certainly pray for healing; I believe Jesus still heals. But there is still more that can be done. The Christian can utilize a redemptive imagination to discover how to interact, comfort, and in some cases, redirect the trajectory of culture toward eradication of disease. While we are not Christ, we are his ambassadors, and, as such, we are to represent his approach toward disease.

Redefine
- If disease is the result of the Fall, who is to blame for its existence in this fallen world? (Hint: The answer is twofold.)

Regain

- How is Face the Nation declaring *this shall not be* concerning the AIDS epidemic in Botswana?
- What does redemption look like to a person with AIDS? What can someone with a terminal disease regain?

Reimagine

- What is Face the Nation doing to imagine their country differently?
- What would it look like if God got his way concerning disease in Botswana? Or the United States?
- How can people suffering with disease be restored, even or especially when there is no cure for their disease? How can a culture suffering with a disease on a large scale be reimagined?

CHAPTER 9

A FATHER IMAGINES FORGIVENESS

It was the type of neighborhood one always saw in movies portraying the perfect everyday life. It was filled with families who had kids of all ages, making it a hodgepodge of activity throughout the entire year. It was the kind of place where neighborhood kids could play in each other's backyards or ride their bikes out on the street. Everyone looked out for everyone else and waved at each other. On any given evening in late spring or summer, the air would be filled with the sound of playing children and the scent of freshly cut grass combined with honeysuckle. Kids could have their entire summers so consumed that the months between May and September were often a blur of adventures and games. Yes, it was a place where time seemed to stand still and fly by simultaneously.

One of the happy families who called this neighborhood home was the Glovers; they had two young girls. I had the privilege of interning for the husband, Dale, who worked as the student pastor of a nearby church. Before this, he had served in the Gulf War where he had seen and experienced things of which he would never speak. Even though he was a small man in stature and the kind of guy who rarely lost his temper, I always had the feeling that just beneath the surface, the warrior was still present. He had emerged from the war convinced of the call that God had placed on his life to serve as a pastor.

Next door lived a very nice family who also had young children, and the Glovers' little girls would go over to their house to play and vice versa. They weren't Christians, which seemed to Dale and his wife like an opportunity to build a relationship and share the gospel. The families would occasionally grill out together, get each other's mail when the other was out of town, and have driveway conversations a few times a week. On the surface, everything seemed fine.

That is until the Glovers' five-year-old daughter began acting quiet and distant following one of her visits to the neighbors' house. Dale and his wife began to ask her what was bothering her in an attempt to find out what was wrong. Eventually, she began to open up and ask her father questions, unusual questions for any child to ask. With each inquiry more was discovered, and eventually enough information was gathered, leaving Dale and his wife with one undeniable conclusion: Their little girl had been molested.

The words *helpless*, *shock*, *anger*, *sadness*, and *disgust* only begin to scratch the surface of the emotion Dale and his wife felt. Dale found himself unable to truly comfort and console his family; he was unable to turn back time, unable to somehow have the insight, and thus unable to protect his daughter's innocence. The internal self-blame certainly seems logical to any man's thinking, much less any father.

The next step was to stop all visits and contact the police. A warrant was issued, an arrest soon followed, and it culminated with a whirlwind of activity that involved interviews, lawyers, and a trial. Dale's neighbor made bail and awaited trial. Every time Dale saw the man's car pull up in the driveway or heard his voice somewhere off in the distance, he would get a deep, nauseous feeling. He immediately put up an eight-foot fence along their property line. After all, this man had abused his little girl, and if they ever came face-to-face, he feared the warrior just beneath the surface, not the pastor, would be unleashed. A couple of weeks went by, and eventually the neighbor's lawyer advised him to temporarily move out of the house.

One day Dale filled up the gas tank on his little push lawn mower and began to cut the grass in his backyard. There was a portion of the fence where he could see over into his neighbor's yard, and suddenly, when he neared that area, the mower just quit. Dale rechecked the gas tank and confirmed it was full; he began to tinker with the motor in a clueless effort to somehow get it working again. He pulled and pulled the rope to crank it and the darn thing wouldn't so much as turn over. Then, to hear Dale explain it, "The Lord spoke to me as clear as I am speaking to you right now. He reminded me in a clear, small voice, 'What has this man done to you that you have not done to my Son?'"

Dale sat down in the uncut grass and began to weep. He realized he hadn't forgiven his enemy, even though the Lord had given him everything necessary to do so. "I just sat in the middle of my backyard and wept like a baby for two hours, and then I got up with another direction from the Lord — forgiveness."

When Dale stood to his feet, he could see into his neighbor's backyard, which hadn't been cut for weeks. He began to ponder what would be a tangible way to express forgiveness. His imagination led him to push his little lawn mower over into the neighbor's yard. He reached down and pulled the rope, and it cranked immediately! Dale said, "The providence of God caused my mower to stop and not restart in my backyard so I could listen to his still, small voice." It seemed impossible, "but with God, all things are possible."

So Dale began to cut the tall grass in his neighbor's back-yard. At the end of one row, he prayed for the children who had lived in that house: "Lord, they are going to need you to be a father to the fatherless." Down the next row, he prayed for the man's wife: *Lord, I can't even begin to understand the pain she must feel. Give her a community of Christian women who will surround her with the love of Jesus.* At the end of another, he prayed for the salvation of the man who had molested his daughter. With each passing row, the father who imagined forgiveness experienced peace.

From that moment on, the tragedy of child abuse would be replaced with a testimony of forgiveness. During the trial the entire courtroom sat in shock as Dale spoke directly to the accused and said, "You don't have an enemy in me. In the name of Jesus, I forgive you." The man never looked at Dale directly, even as he spoke grace and truth over him.

The man would be sentenced to jail time, and his life would, of course, never be the same. During his incarceration he corre-sponded with Dale—and to everyone's astonishment, includ-ing his own, Dale reciprocated. An ongoing conversation began to take place. Dale recently told me that two years into the man's sentence, he opened his heart to Jesus. Thus, one of the most horrendous situations imaginable for a parent ended with God being glorified. When a lifetime of pain and regret seemed inevitable, the explicit command of God to forgive and love even our enemies, coupled with a redemptive imagination, offered a different outcome.

Now, many years later, as Dale recalls the story to me for the glory of God, his daughter is happily married and has also made him a proud grandfather. You see, the story God has told is the one true story, the gospel, and it shall never unravel in the face of tragedy. My friend Dale knows this differently than I probably ever will. He was the warrior who became a father who became a pastor who refused to become a victim, but chose instead to redemptively reimagine what it would look like if God got his way.

ENGAGE

Jesus loves the little children,
All the children of the world.
Red and yellow, black and white,
All are precious in his sight,
Jesus loves the little children of the world.

These words were written by a preacher named Clare Herbert Woolston (1856–1927) and put to the 1864 civil war tune "Tramp! Tramp! Tramp!" by George Frederick Root. Woolston's words were inspired by Matthew 19:14, in which Jesus said, "Let the little children come to me and do not hinder them, for to such belongs the kingdom of heaven." As Woolston expressed in this age-old classic, children matter to the heart of God. This much is undeniable. Earlier in Matthew 18:5-6 we read, "Whoever receives one such child in my name receives me, but whoever causes one of these little ones who believe in me, but whoever causes one of these little ones who believe in me to sin, it would be better for him to have a great millstone fastened around his neck and to be drowned in the depth of the sea." It is obvious in Jesus' ministry that he welcomed children but also that he militantly desired that they be protected.

This language is harsh, and the context in which Jesus is teaching is helpful for understanding just how strongly he felt. He was in Capernaum, a city located along the northwest side of the Sea of Galilee; it has been excavated and can be visited today. A few years ago, on my first visit to the Holy Land, I spent a couple of hours in Capernaum visiting the ruins. Here you can see an excavated millstone, which is a round stone with a hole in the center used for grinding corn; this one weighs a couple hundred pounds. Millstones were a familiar sight in those days. In fact, drowning by millstone was a punishment used by Syrians, Romans, Macedonians, and Greeks, although never the Jews. This sentence was reserved for the worst class of criminals, especially on parricides, one who murders his or her mother, father, or near relative.[1] To the Jew, drowning was a symbol of utter destruction.[2] So when Jesus illustrated his lesson with what would have been considered the cruelest form of punishment, used by some of the cruelest people in the world, his Jewish audience understood clearly the severity of hurting children.

Yet this is the same Jesus who commands his followers in Matthew 5:44 to "love your enemies." It's an impossible request, at first glance, when your enemy is a child molester. Impossible, that is, unless you understand the term *love*, taken from the Greek word *agape*. C. S. Lewis wrote,

> *Charity* means love. It is called Agape in the New Testament to distinguish it from Eros (sexual love), Storage (family affection) and

Philia (friendship). So there are 4 kinds of love, all good in their proper place, but Agape is the best because it is the kind God has for us and is good in all circumstances.[3]

Agape means that no matter how I am treated, abused, grieved, or injured, I will not allow bitterness, anger, or unforgiveness to invade my heart. It means that I will seek the highest good for the person who has committed these actions toward me.

Therefore, when my friend Dale stood in court and proclaimed, "You don't have an enemy in me. In the name of Jesus, I forgive you," he was consistent with both the millstone and *agape*. He was consistent with the millstone in that the court would punish the criminal, but *agape* in that he would love his enemy. When he cut his neighbor's grass he showed a tangible expression of "love your enemies," and it is that expression in which the imagination comes into play.

Redefine
- Child abuse of any kind is the result of fallen people violating God's desire and attitude for children. Therefore, how should children be viewed? How should those who abuse children be viewed? In answering these questions, please take time to search the Scriptures and revisit God's design for the family in the creation plot movement.

Regain
- Following the tragedy of abuse, what did Dale need to regain? What did he declare *shall not be* with the event in his backyard?

- What can a church do to declare abuse *shall not be* in its community?

Reimagine

- How did Dale reimagine his situation? What did his actions declare about *how he would now live*?
- Unfortunately, the abuse of children seems to occur frequently in communities all around us and often appears in news headlines. Think of a recent tragedy and discuss ways the outcome or fallout could be different if one used a redemptive imagination.

CHAPTER 10

THE DAY THE BULLIED DIED

Alisha was always a little weird, even according to her middle school classmates' standards. Being different didn't bother her, and she'd had a steady group of friends throughout much of her elementary school years. But middle school was a different ball game altogether. To the best anyone can tell, it all started to go downhill in the seventh grade, and, more specifically, in the cafeteria. Seventh graders were allowed to choose their seats in a certain part of the lunchroom, and with this new freedom came the birth of cliques or groups of friends jockeying for prominence based on popularity. At the end of lunch, each student was required to return his or her lunch tray to a window where the dishwasher was located.

Alisha had a few friends who all congregated at a certain table. The one thing they all had in common was the fact that they had nothing in common with anyone else. They were the outcasts of what was considered seventh-grade cool. Pretty soon they all began referring to their table as "the island of misfit toys," a reference to the low-budget animated movie *Rudolph, the Red-Nosed Reindeer* and the place where all the defective or unwanted toys were sent. It seemed to categorize the group well and also give them a reason to eat lunch together. Then one day, Alisha was returning her tray to the window when she slipped on some spilled substance. Her legs went out from under her, and up went her tray, along with half an uneaten pizza slice, a little bowl of salad, and some chocolate milk. The moments between her falling flat on her back and the landing of the food on her face seemed to slow down. By the time it was all over, it looked like her lunch had exploded on her face, shirt, and frizzy red hair.

As she lay there with her pride hurting more than her backside, no one came to her aid. Instead, the entire lunchroom burst out in a combination of applause, laughter, and heckling. In the midst of it all, someone yelled out, "Pizza-face!" It's amazing how some names stick, no matter how stupid and juvenile. Such was the case with Alisha, as every day following, when she returned her lunch tray, someone would shout out "Pizza-face!" and the entire room would burst into applause and laughter. The teachers tried to put a stop to it; they stood in strategic positions while Alisha returned her tray. But inevitably someone in the sea of seventh graders would burst out, "Pizza-face!" and all would laugh. Sometimes the culprit would be caught, and other times the entire room would receive verbal warnings and even collective punishment. It didn't matter; the attention seemed to add fuel to the fire.

Even Alisha's "misfit" friends didn't come to her aid, not really. They didn't run to her the day she fell, they didn't walk with her to return her tray, and any encouragement they offered upon her daily return to the island seemed hollow and spineless. In the seventh grade, in a large public school, Alisha was alone.

Her eighth-grade year passed by fairly uneventfully. Though her parents had been made aware of the seventh-grade incident, they simply thought, *Kids are cruel, and now it's over.* Alisha had a fairly good home life with parents who loved her very much, even if they were unaware of how she felt every day at school. Her father worked hard; when he came home, he was usually disengaged as he sat in his chair with a beer and watched the news as he waited for dinner. Her mom, on the other hand, always asked about her day.

In the eighth grade, Alisha showed interest in painting, so her mom surprised her one day by converting an extra bedroom—with a window that offered great light—into a studio. It was one of the greatest gifts she would ever receive. No matter what kind of day she was having, she could always retreat to her studio and get lost in a painting for hours. It was her escape; it turned out she was a pretty gifted artist.

When it was time to go to high school, Alisha's parents needed her to start riding the bus. The middle school had been on her mom's way to work, so for three years her mom had dropped her off and picked her up. But high school was in another direction, and it was easiest for her parents if she rode the bus to and from school each day.

Alisha *hated* riding the bus and dreaded it with an unexplainable revulsion. She felt as if everything bad that could happen did so on the bus ride to and from school. It was on the bus that she saw her first handgun, pornography, and racism and heard every foul joke and word under the sun. It was a yellow cage filled with middle school and high school kids who, for that thirty-minute ride, had no moral compass.

It was a bad place. A girl might be picked on or beat up for sitting in the wrong seat, laughing at the wrong joke, or even sometimes for doing nothing at all. It was survival of the fittest, and this skinny little frizzy-headed ninth grader wasn't very fit. Some days she tried to fit in, and some days she tried to go unnoticed. Some days she was picked on, and some days she slipped by unscathed.

Her parents were uninformed, and she felt no reason to enlighten them. *What's the point?* she thought. In tenth grade the terror from the bus rides spilled over onto the school campus. It was about the same time that everyone was utilizing the new world of social media. As with most high schools across the country, the fascination with Facebook took off like wildfire on her campus. Alisha joined in, creating a profile and accepting friend requests. That was part of the craze; everyone was friends with everyone—even if they weren't.

During the Christmas break of her tenth-grade year, things took a dramatic turn. The combination of free time and free access to everyone at school—without a moral authority looking on—was a recipe for disaster. Questions such as "Who is the hottest girl in school?" start floating around. Following this question, girls starting posting the most flattering pictures of themselves they could find, usually ones involving a bikini and a beach. The questions continued, fostering more contests or games. The questions were at times raunchy, and the comments and pictures that followed always drew an online crowd.

Then after a week or so, the questions turned from vaguely pornographic to vicious. The questions starting revolving around who was the ugliest, fattest, biggest loser, and most likely to be homeless. It was one of these questions that drew considerable attention to Alisha. Someone submitted a question,

Who is the most likely to be an ugly lesbian? A few candidates were nominated, but when Alisha's name was thrown in the hat, the slippery slope of ridicule began all over again.

Someone posted a less-than-flattering yearbook picture of Alisha with a caption that read, "Ugliest lesbian in our high school?" Within a matter of hours, it had more than 250 "likes." It was easy to pick on her; she had no friends and she was weird, so everyone looked at her as a thing instead of a person. This wasn't a cafeteria or a school bus; it was a medium in which nothing was personal. But it was personal to Alisha, who monitored the conversation from her bedroom during what was supposed to be the happiest time of the year. Her parents had no idea; no one's parents did. They didn't even know what social media was; Facebook was brand-new and had just spilled over from the university to high school campuses. The second semester of her tenth-grade year was brutal. A small group of girls began initiating a combination of cyber and face-to-face bullying. Everyone saw the postings and hallway practical jokes. The group even painted "Pizza-face" on her locker one day.

When school let out for summer, Alisha felt as if she could never return to those halls. She was at the end of her rope and was determined never to be humiliated again. People often wonder why the one being bullied doesn't just flee. But Alisha knew, as all bullied children know, that the bullies will still be there tomorrow and the next day and the day after that. There was nowhere to run; there was no escape. During the summer months, while her parents were at work, she stayed up late and watched movies, slept in, and spent hours in her studio. It wasn't a bad routine, except more and more often, the laughter, ridicule, and comments from Facebook rang loud inside her head, even when she was in her studio. It had been a place to escape, but now even her sanctuary was haunted by the ghosts of her past. One day, she'd had enough.

When her mother arrived home from work, she called out to Alisha, "Sweetheart, I'm home!" Usually there was a response, but today there was no reply, only silence. She thought Alisha might be asleep, so she cracked the door to her room, only to see an empty bed. Then she made her way down the hall to Alisha's studio. When she opened the door she discovered her little artist, her baby girl, had hung herself on the beam that ran horizontally across the old closet that had been a studio for the last three years. Her mother ran to her lifeless body in a futile attempt to save her daughter. It was too late; Alisha had been dead for hours. She collapsed on the floor and wept uncontrollably. At one point she looked up and through the tears saw something clipped to Alisha's easel. There were her daughter's final words.

ALONE: one last reflection
The shadows are closing all around
The demons and voices with their penetrating sound
The halls of humiliation I will now leave behind
The days of misery have now crossed a line
I bear the burdens that no one knows
Wearing my heart just beneath my clothes

The world once big now appears small
The girl inside no longer stands tall
When moments of gloom become the norm
When the theme of fear is a lasting storm
Options are gone, no hero will arrive
I cannot go on, I cannot survive

Kindness went on vacation and never came back
It doesn't matter I wouldn't trust its track
Love is a myth that cannot come true
Love is a debt that is overdue

I am young but this story is old
At the start with finish foretold
The credits of my narrative will have a full cast
The only comfort I have is they are the past
The future is nothing or at best unknown
So I leave this life the way I experienced it . . . alone

ENGAGE

Alisha is a true fictitious character. By that I mean she is a compilation of many sad and tragic stories that have made headlines over the last several years. I also admit I've used my personal experience being bullied on a school bus to create Alisha's character.

Make no mistake, she is as real as you or I, and she is present on every middle school and high school campus in the country. *The Bully Project* defines bullying this way:

Bullying is a widespread and serious problem that can happen anywhere. It is not a phase children have to go through, it is not "just messing around" and it is not something we just grow out of. Bullying can cause serious and lasting harm. Although definitions of bullying vary, most agree that bullying involves:

- *Imbalance of power:* people who bully use their power to control or harm, and the people being bullied may have a hard time defending themselves.
- *Intent to cause harm:* actions done by accident are not bullying; the person bullying has a goal to cause harm.
- *Repetition:* incidents of bullying happen to the same person over and over by the same person or group.[1]

The many forms of bullying include verbal, social, physical, and cyber, all of which can be seen in Alisha's story. There is no doubt in my mind that bullying breaks the heart of God and should be viewed as sinful behavior. The term *ungodly* simply means to act as if God's standards did not exist. Bullying is in direct violation to how the Bible commands us to treat people:

- You shall not hate your brother in your heart, but you shall reason frankly with your neighbor, lest you incur sin because of him. You shall not take vengeance or bear a grudge against the sons of your own people, but you shall love your neighbor as yourself: I am the LORD. (Leviticus 19:17-18)
- You shall love the Lord your God with all your heart and with all your soul and with all your strength and with all your mind, and your neighbor as yourself. (Luke 10:27)
- He has told you, O man, what is good; and what does the LORD require of you but to do justice, and to love kindness, and to walk humbly with your God? (Micah 6:8)
- Do nothing from selfish ambition or conceit, but in humility count others more significant than yourselves. (Philippians 2:3)

- Let no one seek his own good, but the good of his neighbor. (1 Corinthians 10:24)
- Give no offense to Jews or to Greeks or to the church of God, just as I try to please everyone in everything I do, not seeking my own advantage, but that of many, that they may be saved. (1 Corinthians 10:32-33)

The bully is in direct violation of each one of these verses; he is acting as if God's standards do not exist. The bully tears down, looks out for himself, offends, is selfish, hates, and in no way loves kindness or justice. Yet the Christian is called to build up others, care for others as more important, and champion the cause of what is right and just. In his work *Concerning Christian Liberty*, the great Reformer Martin Luther wrote, "That all our works should be directed to the advantage of others, since every Christian has such abundance through his faith that all his other works and his whole life remain over and above wherewith to serve and benefit his neighbor of spontaneous good will."[2] He would additionally emphasize his point: "A Christian man is the most free lord of all, and subject to none; a Christian man is the most dutiful servant of all, and subject to every one."[3]

Alisha's story has a tragic ending. My hope is that your heart longs for it to have ended differently. This, of course, brings us to a point at which we attempt to employ a redemptive imagination that allows for a God-glorifying outcome.

Redefine
- Identify the many parts of this story that *ought not be*. (Hint: Some are much more obvious than others.)

- Think about someone you have seen bullied, or maybe you have personal experience. What emotions must the bullied feel? How is his or her view of self altered as a result of being victimized?

Regain

- There are three identifiable events in Alisha's life (the cafeteria, the bus, Facebook), and each one served to de-create her life even more than the former, taking her from a creative and fun-loving young girl to one consumed with self-loathing and fear. Because this story has a tragic ending, how could it be retold?
- What message could some followers of Christ have declared to Alisha? How could they have comforted her with *this shall not be*?

Reimagine

- Reimagine Alisha's story as if a group of Christians gathered around her to comfort and protect her (redeem) from the bully. What could that group have done to offer her God-honoring relationships?
- Dreamcast how Alisha's story could be retold.

CHAPTER 11

A STROKE OF INSPIRATION

Derrick was a portrait of health and loved his role as pastor. He had a balanced diet, exercised three to four times a week, and seemed to manage the responsibilities and stress of being a pastor well. He and his wife were empty nesters, and recently one of their daughters had made them proud grandparents. Both in their midfifties, life seemed to be going pretty much according to plan. They had a great marriage and kids, good jobs, and a wonderful home located in North Carolina. They loved where they lived because the mountains and the beach were both within driving distance.

For Christmas last year, Derrick gave his wife the trip of a lifetime. She had a particular fascination with photography, and as a wedding gift twenty-five years earlier, he had given her a camera. Young, in love, and childless, they had discussed road trips to picturesque locations that she could photograph.

The gift itself had been marinating in Derrick's brain for

years, causing him to plan even the smallest of details. For example, he printed copies of a newspaper article from *USA Today* titled "The Ten Most Beautiful Places in America" and used it as wrapping paper for the new camera he had bought her. He wrapped the camera under ten layers of pictures and descriptions of locations. As she carefully opened the present Christmas morning, she worked her way through every destination: Red Rock country in Sedona, Arizona; a nighttime view from Mount Washington in Pittsburgh; a beautiful spot along the upper portion of the Mississippi River; Hawaii's Na Pali Coast; the Golden Gate Bridge in San Francisco; the foothills in Grafton, Vermont; Jenny Lake in Grand Teton National Park, Wyoming; the Florida Keys; Clingmans Dome along the Appalachian Trail in Great Smoky Mountains National Park; and the squares of Savannah, Georgia.

As his wife unwrapped the box, she thought her husband was just being funny; she had no idea what he had planned and had in no way begun to connect the dots. Inside was a brand-new camera, an incredibly thoughtful gift indeed, but when she lifted it out of the box, there underneath was a single piece of paper. When she picked it up it read across the top, "Ten trips . . . Ten weeks . . . Ten most beautiful places in America for the most beautiful wife in the world." A combination of shock and gratitude flooded her emotions. She would have so many questions, such as "How can we afford this?" and "How can we take that much time away from work?" To each he had a well-prepared answer. They had lived on a budget for twenty-five years, and on the side he had been saving for quite some time. Additionally, the church had given him a six-month sabbatical for his twenty-year anniversary as their pastor. As the shock subsided, the excitement took over and Christmas morning sounded more like childlike celebration than two adults in their fifties.

The trip was planned to begin at the end of the summer, giving both of them a good six to seven months to plan and prepare. It also gave them lots of time to anticipate and have conversations that reminded them both of their early days as husband and wife. When July finally arrived they set off on their adventure of a lifetime.

The first three weeks were as magical as either one of them could have ever imagined. Early in the fourth week, while spending some time in San Francisco, Derrick started having sudden severe headaches that seemed to come out of nowhere. He took pain reliever and continued on, not desiring to interrupt the adventure. One morning toward the end of the week, his vision started blurring and he began to experience a tingling sensation in his face. Now that it had moved beyond headaches, he told his wife, who immediately rushed him to the hospital. By the time they arrived in the emergency room, Derrick was having trouble speaking and moving his left leg and arm. Even with his wife's quick response and the best efforts of the medical staff, the effects were temporarily irreversible: Derrick had suffered a stroke.

Life seemed to suddenly stand still. Life seemed to suddenly not make sense. The next couple of weeks were spent in the ICU surrounded by his wife and kids. At times he could think clearly; other times he could not, and a wave of emotion would come over him as he cried uncontrollably. It was as if he had aged suddenly and left behind a body that only worked on the right side. In one sense, it was humiliating, not even being able to go the bathroom or eat without help. In another sense, to be surrounded by so much love and care from family was encouraging. The left side of his face was completely paralyzed, along with his arm and leg, making communication either difficult or next to impossible.

From the moment the doctor said he was stable enough to leave ICU for a normal room, only one question mattered: How much of his faculties would he regain? The doctor assured Derrick's wife and kids that while some tests could help with answering that question, only time would yield the final outcome. The doctor assured them the best thing for Derrick was to begin therapy as soon as possible. Derrick's wife decided they would stay in California and begin therapy. One ray of hope was that this hospital had one of the best therapy centers for stroke victims in the state. He was immediately moved to the top floor to begin therapy and work toward a full recovery.

Unfortunately, the days would turn into weeks and the weeks into months with very little progress. Derrick felt like he was experiencing a steady dose of frustration and stalled progress. After a few months and a lot of grace from their insurance company, Derrick, his wife, and one of their daughters began to drive back across the country to North Carolina. It was now late October, and it had been over three months since Derrick wasn't bound to a hospital.

Several days later, they arrived home to a new reality. Their home was two stories, and a few years ago they had finished their basement to provide Derrick with a home office where he could study and write. Their two daughters' rooms had been upstairs and the master bedroom, kitchen, dining room, and living room were on the ground level. This was the house Derrick remembered.

As they pulled into the driveway and the garage door opened, Derrick's new reality began to take shape. The stairs leading from the garage to the kitchen had been replaced with a ramp. For nearly twenty years he had walked up those stairs; now he needed help getting out of the car and into a wheelchair. Once inside, Derrick saw the entire ground floor had been remodeled, making room for his wheelchair to travel from room to room. It felt like he was entering his home for the first time. His wife had had so much work done to prepare for his arrival home, and he didn't want to appear disappointed or ungrateful, but it didn't matter. He couldn't hold back the tears; the house in its present state seemed to scream, "Defeat!"

Derrick pulled himself together and tried to block out thoughts of being worthless and pathetic. He desperately didn't want to entertain the questions that seemed to haunt his thinking: "Will I ever hold my wife again? Will I ever be able to preach and pastor my church again?"

Maybe his wife knew the thoughts he would be struggling with; maybe she had anticipated the bad days. In any case, she pushed the chair to where the dining room had previously been, and they turned the corner to a room transformed into his study. Up to this point the house seemed to remind him of defeat—now the message was one of reimagined possibilities and hope.

She had gone to careful lengths to replicate the office from the basement. The layout of the rooms was similar, making possible the identical placement of bookshelves, lamps, coffeemaker, and desk. He turned his head and reached up with his right arm to pull her face to his. In his darkest moment since the stroke, she had opened a window and let the light in. With their faces touching cheek-to-cheek, he whispered a simple "Thank you," and she whispered back, "Why don't you give it a test run?" With his right arm, he positioned his chair behind his desk. The vision in his left eye was the only faculty he had regained, but it was enough. There on the desk was a sermon he had been working on before they left for their adventure of a lifetime.

He looked at his chicken-scratch handwriting on a yellow legal pad. He was going to preach a series about the sufficiency of Christ, and this was to be the opening sermon. Written across the top of the page were the words *Text: Colossians 3:11 — Title: Out of Heaven and into Us — Central idea: Christ is everything I need for justification, sanctification, and glorification.* The title of the sermon was actually the title of one of the devotionals from a book called *The Indwelling Life of Christ,* by Major W. Ian Thomas. Derrick had planned on quoting from the devotional and written out two quotes from the book:

- The Lord Jesus came from heaven to earth not just to get us out of hell and into heaven — though He is the only One who can and does, if we let Him — but to get Himself out of heaven and into us.[1]
- Christ did not die simply that you might be saved from a bad conscience, or even to remove the stain of past failure, but to "clear the decks" for His divine activity through you.[2]

The words of Scripture felt like home to him as he reflected on the part of the verse that reads, "Christ is all and in all." They wrapped around him like a warm blanket offering comfort and encouragement. All the while, his wife stood in the doorway and observed the man of God she fell in love with so many years ago, now standing as tall as ever in her mind.

Derrick ended up having to resign from his church because

he was unable to execute his tasks as senior pastor. No one wanted his departure, and in the end it was his decision. But this wasn't the end of the story, just the completion of a chapter. He would go on disability, and his wife would only be able to work part-time because of the responsibility of taking care of her husband. He would continue in therapy with very little progress.

Each day would begin the same way it always had, even before the stroke, with a hot cup of coffee and an open Bible in his study. Even though he was no longer behind the pulpit, Derrick still wrote sermons on legal pads and typed them on his computer. Just because he wasn't preaching didn't mean he could just turn off the twenty-five-year habit of preparing sermons. Each day he would check his e-mail; there were always several blogs he enjoyed reading each week from pastors and evangelical leaders he respected.

One day while he was reading blogs, an interesting idea occurred: *I can do this. I can write a blog.* He leaned back in his chair and allowed his thoughts to run wild with the idea. Pretty soon he began thinking of a title and series he could write. He filled up two sheets on his legal pad with ideas and across the first page wrote, "Sermons Without Sound."

When his wife came in mid-morning to check on Derrick, she noticed an excitement that hadn't been there for some time. She took a seat and listened as he explained he wanted to post a sermon on a blog. His thought was that there were thousands of pastors every week who were unable to take in a sermon because they were so busy preparing the one they would deliver the next Sunday. He also thought people who would never step into a church might consider reading a blog. On and on his idea evolved, on and on his imagination began to fill in the gaps between his calling and his disability.

That was several years ago. Today Derrick preaches weekly to a congregation that is several thousand large; every week at least a hundred people reach out to him for pastoral care and counsel. In one sense, the stroke limited Derrick for the rest of his life, but in another sense, it served as a catalyst for a redemptive imagination. And the sermon series on the sufficiency of Christ became the theme of Derrick's story and all his sermons. If you could talk to him now and ask him about his message, he would give you a half smile and say, "Christ is all, and in all."

ENGAGE

Jesus can heal any disease or ailment. Jesus does heal, but not always. We know the Lord offers healing, but we also know he can bring about what we would consider tragedy. This is a tough pill to swallow for some of us, but Isaiah 45:7 states, "I form light and create darkness, I make well-being and create calamity, I am the LORD, who does all these things."

Many translators rightly use the word *evil* instead of *calamity*. This is not to say God creates moral evil or evil of sin (God is not the author of that); evil here refers to punishment.[3] I agree with the following commentator's interpretation of this text:

> Jehovah is the Creator and Sustainer of the physical universe, and of the moral law as well. The *evil* he creates is the antithesis of *peace*. But since the opposite of peace is not sin or moral evil, it is obvious that physical evil, or the calamitous consequences of wrongdoing are here intended. Nowhere does the Scripture ascribe to God the creation

or authorship of sin; this originates only from the free moral agency of created beings.[4] (emphasis added)

Questions such as "Why did God allow this to happen to me?" can, at times, do more harm than help. There is no way to step inside the brain of almighty God and see his decreed will; after all, it is hidden from us, as we have discussed. It is important to remember, "We don't yet see things clearly. We're squinting in a fog, peering through a mist. But it won't be long before the weather clears and the sun shines bright! We'll see it all then, see it all as clearly as God sees us, knowing him directly just as he knows us!" (1 Corinthians 13:12, MSG).

Derrick receives great medical care and continues to go to therapy, but he will probably never regain the use of his left leg and arm. But this doesn't mean the call of God is removed from his life; it just means he has to discover another way to serve. This is where the role of imagination comes into play.

Redefine
- Derrick serves as an incredible example of a redemptive imagination at work. How could he have reacted to the stroke differently? What negative mind-set and emotions could he have entertained? In other words, what are some hypothetical *ought-not-be* situations that could have occurred?

Regain
- What statement does Derrick make with his response to the stroke? How did he reflect the four plot movements with the story his life told?

Reimagine

- How did Derrick reimagine his life after he came home from the hospital?
- How can someone with a debilitating condition be brought out (redeemed) of a place where he or she is not functioning and put into a place where he or she is contributing (restored)? How can this be accomplished when someone has suffered a stroke or some other debilitating condition like severe arthritis or muscular dystrophy?

CHAPTER 12

LORD SAVE THE COUNTRY BOY

Jesse was like most other kids who lived in the country. He loved trucks, hunting, and the great outdoors. It was a rural community not yet infiltrated by subdivisions and strip malls at every intersection with a stoplight. People here knew each other—and if they didn't, they still waved as they drove past each other on the street. The drugstore was still family-owned, and one could fuel up the car, eat a meal, and get a haircut all at the same place. Most of the men awaited the opening of deer season like a little child anticipates Christmas. This is where Jesse lived, and he liked it. He liked being able to see more land than buildings. He liked the open sky at night and witnessing all the stars on parade. Yes sir, he was a country boy and proud of it!

His family rarely went to church but considered themselves good people. They would have considered themselves Christian, certainly, pointing to their good works and heritage; after all, Christian was something you were because of your parents. Jesse's father was a hard worker who owned his own carpet-cleaning business; his mother was the receptionist at the local doctor's office. They were a blue-collar, yellow-dog Democrat family everyone respected. They also lived on the property next door to my family.

My dad pastored the local Baptist church, and I attended the one high school in the county. We had moved to this little community from . . . well, let's just say a less rural place. The country was literally a breath of fresh air and full of new opportunities for someone who had never lived outside a subdivision before. In school I was a couple of years ahead of Jesse, so our paths never had a reason to cross. We lived on a seven-acre plot of land that stopped where his family's ten-acre spread started. The only thing we shared was a fence and the occasional wave driving past each other on the gravel road.

I remember the Christmas when Jesse's parents gave him an all-terrain vehicle, commonly referred to as an ATV or a four-wheeler. It seems that there wasn't an afternoon that would go by that he wasn't riding that thing up and down our gravel road and off-road throughout the wide-open country. An ATV was a necessary luxury for extracurricular activities like deer hunting or fishing. If one were to kill a deer, the ATV was quite helpful to get the carcass out of the forest and into a garage where it could be cleaned. Or if one were to go fishing deep in the woods, the ATV could be used to transport all the equipment needed and return with a cooler full of fish in a fraction of the time it would take to walk. When Jesse wasn't busy hunting or fishing, he could be seen joyriding with his girlfriend up and down the back roads where we lived.

During my senior year in high school, I returned home one day to what I thought was an empty house. The lights were off, so I was surprised to walk into the dimly lit kitchen to discover my father just sitting at the table. He asked me to take a seat so we could talk. It all seemed a bit out of the ordinary, but I pulled up a chair.

"Do you know the kid next door?" my father asked.

I replied, "He's a couple years younger than me, but yes, Jesse. Everyone knows who he is because he is always riding that four-wheeler."

"Well, he won't be riding it anymore," my dad said. "This afternoon he had an accident. He flipped it, and when he fell off, he broke his neck and died instantly." At that moment, I felt a deep but also distant sadness come over me. It was deep because my heart immediately broke for his parents, who had just lost their only child, but it was distant because I didn't have a personal relationship with Jesse.

My father's next words were meant to be reflective, though they served a much more poignant purpose as he spoke them. "You know, I have preached the gospel for years, I have held evangelistic events at our church and urged people to invite their neighbors, I have taken hundreds of church members on overseas mission trips, but I never went next door. I never told Jesse about Jesus." He was speaking about his own life, but he could just as easily have been speaking about mine. I had grown up in a godly home, had a personal relationship with Jesus, had gone on several mission trips, and had been involved in my youth group. I had done a lot and at the same time felt like I had accomplished nothing by way of obedience. Not only did I never share Jesus with Jesse, it never even occurred to me. Here was an infinitely valuable person in need of the grace of God, but all I saw was a redneck kid who was always making a bunch of noise with his four-wheeler.

There was an age difference, we had grown up differently, and because of where we lived there weren't those chance meetings that happen when taking out the trash or going to the mailbox. There were a lot of excuses and very little, if any, imagination to discover a way to form a relationship and share the greatest story ever told.

For the last ten years, I have had more opportunities than I could have ever envisioned preaching at church services, conferences, concerts, and festivals. People are always coming up to me afterward and telling me how well I did, whether they mean it or not, or how their life was changed or that they placed their faith in Christ at an event where I was preaching. It is incredibly encouraging, to say the least, when someone relates how God spoke to him and you were privileged to serve in the process. Almost every week I get on a plane, get in a rental car, sleep in a hotel, and preach at an event. I don't say that to sound important, because if you have ever spent time on the road with your vocation, you know there is nothing glamorous about prepackaged cereal and canceled flights. The reason I give you a glimpse into my weekly comings and goings is because no matter how many people have given their life to Christ over the last ten years or will in the next ten, Jesse is still in hell.

I don't live with guilt, as I have asked for and experienced God's forgiveness. I do live with a regret. I regret I never took the time to imagine a way to share the gospel with Jesse. I don't mean I live in the past; instead, I allow that regret to serve as a sacred reminder that we should tell the most compelling story because we, the most undeserving of all, are the most compelled.

So this is my commitment: I will know those who live around me, I will view them as infinitely valuable, and I will point them to Jesus. Will you?

ENGAGE

God doesn't want people to go to hell. Case closed. The Bible is very clear on this point:

- Have I any pleasure in the death of the wicked, declares the Lord GOD, and not rather that he should turn from his way and live? (Ezekiel 18:23)
- This is good, and it is pleasing in the sight of God our Savior, who desires all people to be saved and to come to the knowledge of the truth. (1 Timothy 2:3-4)
- The Lord is not slow to fulfill his promise as some count slowness, but is patient toward you, not wishing that any should perish, but that all should reach repentance. (2 Peter 3:9)

God wants everyone to be saved, but people die without the gift of salvation every day. God wants the story to continue past the Fall toward the promise of redemption, but act two—the second plot movement—is the final for so many. What are we to make of this? God, who could and should get his desires, will have some that go unmet. Dr. Daniel Akin stated it this way in a sermon on 1 Timothy 2:

The Savior God desires (Greek "telei"; wishes, wants) *all* to be saved. The statement is profound in its simplicity. No qualifications. No exceptions. . . . There is a great tension and mystery in all of this, but there is no mystery in the revealed basic, bedrock, biblical truth: God desires all men, all persons, to be saved. This is His heart and this must be our heart. The nations are on His heart. All humanity is on His heart.[1]

With that in mind, think about what the Christian's response to what God wants should be. Not only does God want people to go to heaven, he has chosen and commanded his followers to "Go therefore and make disciples of all nations, baptizing them in the name of the Father and of the Son and of the Holy Spirit, teaching them to observe all that I have commanded you. And behold, I am with you always, to the end of the age" (Matthew 28:19-20). Jesus not only commanded his followers to be evangelizing, disciple-making advancers of his movement, he also served as the great example. There are over forty instances in the Gospels of Jesus confronting people with the kingdom of God.

I often heard Bill Bright define evangelism as "presenting Jesus Christ in the power of the Holy Spirit and leaving the results to God." Evangelizing the lost was a priority to Jesus, is a clear command in Scripture, and something close to the heart of God; there should be but one response from his children: to evangelize the world.

By this I mean that we are to see ourselves strategically involved in the mission of God. In his book *The Mission of God*, Christopher Wright sees even the Bible as a missional phenomenon. He wrote, "The God who walks the paths of history through the pages of the Bible pins a mission statement to every signpost on the way."[2] Some say these missiological passages of the Bible mean the Bible is all about mission. But this "does not mean that we try to find something relevant to evangelism in every verse. We are referring to something deeper and wider in relation to the Bible as a whole. In a missiological approach to the Bible, we are thinking of:

- The purpose for which the Bible exists
- The God the Bible renders to us

- The people whose identity and mission the Bible invites us to share
- The story the Bible tells about God, his people and indeed about the whole world and its future"[3]

Although God is all about his mission, which is evidenced through the existence of and message of his Bible, the question of how to do evangelism as part of God's mission takes central stage. There are many approaches to sharing Jesus; each has strengths and some even have weaknesses. These approaches include personal evangelism through confrontation or a relationship; servanthood evangelism, in which acts of kindness serve as a catalyst to share the good news; event evangelism, in which someone hears the gospel in a large setting; and so on. In the present age of social media, people are finding new and creative ways to share the message of Jesus. In any case, this is where a redemptive imagination is set free to discover and implement ways to build bridges from the lives of those outside the faith to the feet of Jesus.

Redefine
- What *ought not be* in the story about my neighbor Jesse?
- What did I fail to recognize concerning his worth and the mission of God?

Regain
- What *this-shall-not-be* message should my actions have declared?
- If the plot movement of redemption affords mankind a way to regain a relationship with God, how should this

message affect our view of others and our personal
witness?

Reimagine

- Imagine yourself in my shoes in the story about Jesse.
  What would it have looked like to lead Jesse to Jesus?
  Imagine the joy of leading someone to Christ and
  remember the peace you experienced the moment
  you were saved.
- Identify someone in your life who is dead in his
  sins—he is lost and will go to hell if he died right now.
  Now reimagine your interactions with him, working
  through the redemptive imagination process—and act
  on it.

CHAPTER 13

BOYS WHO SHAVE

Nathan Thompson and his wife, Catherine, had two awesome boys and always tried to give them the best. It was a wonderful and happy childhood for five-year-old Dylan and eight-year-old Gabriel. Catherine was able to be a stay-at-home mom while Nathan worked as a lawyer for a small firm. Summers were like a highlight reel, filled with afternoons playing in the backyard, hours in the pool, baked treats, and family vacations to the beach. They had even taken a trip to Disney World that proved to be both magical and exhausting.

During the school year, Catherine was involved at the kids' school, where she served as class mom. She went on field trips, participated in fund-raisers, and helped out with teacher appreciation days. In the evenings, Nathan came home anxious to play with the kids and see his wife. They lived in a nice neighborhood just outside of Atlanta, Georgia, and Nathan's commute each day was manageable, in spite of the heavy traffic. The couple enjoyed the rhythm of their family life to the point that they felt guilty they were so blessed.

Nathan was becoming acutely aware that his life—as a Christian man in his early thirties, trying to be a godly husband and father—was far from the norm. His colleagues at the law firm, even though they were married, seemed strangely determined to relive their youth. There was an ongoing obsession with other women to the point that Nathan would have to discreetly excuse himself from conversations. Every lunch, if there were a female server, would involve flirtatious behavior and juvenile hypotheticals about her when she left. Several of the men were cheating on their wives, and one even had an apartment that his wife didn't know about.

Not only was there a fascination with women other than their wives, these men also had a preoccupation with juvenile hobbies like video games. Sure, Nathan enjoyed the occasional trip to a restaurant that was more game room than anything else or playing a football video game every once in a while. But this was different: The men spent hundreds of dollars on consoles and violent games in which the weapons seemed based on fiction and the carnage appeared real-life. Their knowledge of game minutiae reminded Nathan of his teenage days, when he and his brother had mastered every level of a run-and-gun action game named *Contra*, but only if they knew the secret passcode for extra lives: up-up-down-down-b-a-b-a-select-start.

All of this only served to deepen Nathan's resolve to love his wife as Christ loved the church and to raise his sons "in the discipline and instruction of the Lord" (Ephesians 6:4). More and more Nathan and Catherine were becoming aware of how fast the time with their children was passing. The couple had always heard parents with older kids say things like, "It goes by so fast," and "Just yesterday my kids were their age and now they're driving." But now that Dylan was in preschool and

Gabriel in second grade, the kids growing older was a sobering reality. They even found themselves saying, "It seems like just yesterday they were . . ."

From the beginning, they both had a deeply rooted faith and a holy desperation within their hearts to raise Dylan and Gabriel to be men of God. But how were they to nurture, discipline, and instruct the boys in the way of godliness? As they searched the Scriptures together, they soon discovered there was no shortage of parenting gone wrong. David pampering Absalom, Eli not disciplining his sons, and the divided home of Isaac indulging Esau and his wife showing favoritism to Jacob. One verse seemed to capture the essence of what they wanted to accomplish: "Fathers, do not provoke your children to anger, but bring them up in the discipline and instruction of the Lord" (Ephesians 6:4). All the biblical examples of negative parenting seemed to violate some portion of if not the entire verse. While this verse was part of an entire passage on child-parent relationships, including instruction that the child is to honor and obey his or her parents (Ephesians 6:1-4), verse four is directed to fathers in particular.

Nathan and Catherine knew deep in their hearts that if they mismanaged the parenting of their children, it would be next to impossible for that child to reach his full potential. In fact, the fifth commandment, which is the first commandment with a promise, commands, "Honor your father and your mother, that your days may be long in the land that the LORD your God is giving you" (Exodus 20:12). The failure to parent in a godly way sets the child up for disaster, robbing him of a future blessing, as indicated in the second half of the verse. Their first step, then, was to be godly parents, ones worthy of honoring. This is why Paul instructs parents not to "provoke your children to anger."

How were they to bring up Dylan and Gabriel? To answer this question they would need to first discover the meaning of "bring them up in the discipline and instruction of the Lord." They soon discovered the phrase *bring up* has to do with providing the proper nourishment for the child. This means much more than food; it means to provide for the child what was necessary to be brought up in a godly manner. First, they were to receive *discipline*, which points to the orderly manner in which the child is educated according to the guidelines of a Christian home. This, of course, means the child is to be corrected when he disobeys these guidelines. The second word, *instruction*, literally means "putting in mind." While discipline has more to do with systematic education, instruction seems to focus more on right attitudes and behavior.[1]

Now their attention turned to the question of how to accomplish taking Dylan and Gabriel "by the hand and lead them in the way of the Master" (Ephesians 6:4, MSG). Since there was an emphasis on fatherhood in the text, Nathan led the way. He turned his focus to the kitchen table, of all places. Lately Nathan had been arriving home tired or late, and Catherine would have already fed the kids; when they did sit down for a meal together, the only purpose was, of course, eating. But Nathan was now going to transform the kitchen table into a place for spiritual nourishment for his family.

First, he made a commitment to being home for dinner each night at a reasonable hour, making it possible for them to eat together as a family. At times this meant going into the office an hour early. Other times it would mean that he couldn't take on certain cases, because he had a new priority. Each evening the family would eat a meal together, and Nathan would lead the conversations. Before, mealtime conversations had revolved around whatever came up. Now they were intentional: Nathan was parenting on purpose, even at the dinner table.

The couple wanted to instruct their children about the character or attributes of God. This took some imaginative thinking, particularly when the children were young. They started by discussing a different characteristic of God each night. Other times they focused on memorizing Scripture by putting it to songs and celebrating when a verse was successfully quoted.

Once a week they had a family devotion time in the den. And Nathan made sure to spend one-on-one time with each of his sons. As the boys grew older, their interests changed and Nathan always evolved accordingly. He wanted "guy time" to be his sons' time to have fun and just hang out with their dad. Some of the greatest conversations happened at the end of a fishing dock or walking through an antique car show.

The boys became teenagers about the same time the media began to depict the decay of manhood. A portrait was now being painted for them of boys who shave—adolescent men who can't grow up. The *New York Times* ran an article titled "What Is It About 20-Somethings?" that stated, "The traditional cycle seems to have gone off course, as young people remain untethered to romantic partners or to permanent homes, going back to school for lack of better options, traveling, avoiding commitments, competing ferociously for unpaid internships or temporary (and often grueling) Teach for America jobs, forestalling the beginning of adult life."[2] The article would go on to report that 40 percent of twentysomethings move back in with their parents at least once. How were Nathan and Catherine to have any hope for their sons?

They continued to nourish their sons with Scriptures and focused more on the biblical idea for manhood. Nathan knew that much of the education the boys would receive about manhood would be through his example and their relationship with him. Catherine knew that part of her role in their education was to demonstrate that a godly wife respects her husband as the spiritual leader of the home. It was a joint effort, and they understood their relationship with each other had to reflect the biblical principles they were trying to instill.

When Gabriel turned sixteen, Nathan decided to hold a special ceremony—a banquet and the company of some important men in the boy's life. At the table were Gabriel's grandfather, uncle, youth pastor, two of Nathan's friends from church whom Gabriel was close to, and his soccer coach, who was a strong believer and a constant source of encouragement. Each man was personally invited by Nathan and Catherine with the instruction to bring a letter describing the responsibilities of manhood. The letter was to be read at a designated time during the meal.

It was a wonderful, heartfelt evening, repeated a few years later when Dylan turned sixteen. Each man stood and read his letter. With each message came a different emphasis, but there were also constant themes having to do with integrity and purity. The conversations were rich, the letters were priceless, and the relationships were the classroom for developing each of the boys into godly men. The ceremony sent a clear message: "You are a man, but you must always strive to be a man of God."

Catherine later would put the letters into a special notebook and give them to each of the boys before they left home for college. In the end, Nathan and Catherine focused on enjoying the parenting process by enjoying God. They weren't perfect, no one is, but certainly served as an example to be followed.

ENGAGE

The Bible commands us to raise our children with discipline and instruction in the Lord, and as Christians we are to obey; the bridge between the two is a redemptive imagination. Parenting is as much a work of art guided by biblical principles as anything.

But make no mistake about it, there is a cultural crisis concerning manhood. Darrin Patrick, church planter and vice president of the Acts 29 Church Planting Network, writes about this crisis:

> We live in a world full of males who have prolonged their adolescence. They are neither boys nor men. They live, suspended as it were, between childhood and adulthood, between growing up and being grown-ups. Let's call this kind of male *Ban*, a hybrid of both boy and man. Ban is juvenile because there has been an entire niche created for him to live in the lusts of youth. The accompanying culture not only tolerates this behavior but encourages it and endorses it. (Consider magazines like *Maxim* or movies like *Wedding Crashers*.) This kind of male is everywhere, including the church.[3]

But the movement of Christianity requires a boy to grow up to be a man — not a boy who shaves or a Ban, in Darrin Patrick's verbiage.

Redefine

- How has culture twisted the ideas of womanhood and manhood as a result of living in a fallen world?
- In a culture that has perverted the ideas of womanhood and manhood, how must these ideas be redefined in light of what Scripture teaches?
- What ought a God-honoring love story look like?

Regain

- What needs to be regained in order to fulfill the divine purpose for manhood and womanhood? What *this-shall-not-be* message are we to send concerning these issues?

Reimagine

- In light of how you have answered the previous questions, how should we now live?
- What are some creative ways to foster and champion the idea of biblical womanhood or manhood? (Answer this from your current perspective: parent, son, daughter, single, married without children.)

CHAPTER 14

A COURAGEOUS IMAGINATION

Michael had always felt that there was something odd about him and his family, that there was an untold story hovering just beneath the surface. The idea of a secret story was only enhanced by how his extended family treated him. It's not that they were cruel; they were just distant, regarding him more like an outsider than anything else.

For example, most children have memories of spending the night at their grandparents' house; it's usually their first experience sleeping somewhere other than home and leaves a lasting impression on young children. Maybe it's the way Grandma's house smells or a certain food that is always served. The best grandparents harness this, using it to make wonderful, lifelong imprints in the hearts of their grandkids.

These are the memories one is supposed to have, but such memories were void from Michael's childhood. His father's parents, in particular, kept him at arm's length relationally. As a little boy, not yet old enough to construct conspiracy theories about being adopted, he simply wondered, "What is wrong with me?"

As the years went by, Michael's childhood experiences, coupled with a maturing mind, occasionally gave him pause. He discovered that his mother had given birth to a little girl who died during World War II and had also, around that same time, been diagnosed with Bright's disease. Bright's disease is a historic and thus broad classification of kidney disease and, in recent years, the phrase isn't used much in the medical field as they have further specified different types of kidney conditions. But it didn't take much research for Michael to discover that most women with Bright's disease were unable to get pregnant. Over the years there were other signs, such as the fact that his mother, father, and most of his family were introverts and yet Michael was an extrovert. The whole experience, to hear him describe it, "just felt odd at times."

When I was speaking to Michael, he was very quick to point out that while his parents were not particularly spiritual people, they were very good to him and raised him in a moral environment. Their approach to their faith was, unfortunately, like many in evangelical churches: very compartmentalized. This was a lifestyle Michael would emulate throughout his teenage years. No matter how ungodly the behavior on Saturday night, come Sunday morning he was present for church. It is an incredible and enduring principle that stands the test of time and culture: The loudest message heard is the example that is set. The life lived before children sets a pattern of behavior in their lives that will potentially affect generations to come.

Growing up in church, he had made a profession of faith during vacation Bible school one summer, but it wasn't until age nineteen, on a youth church trip, of all places, that he would truly find a life in Jesus. The trip was to Panama City Beach on the panhandle of Florida. One afternoon the youth group was out doing personal evangelism. Michael had a great mind and thus had the presentation and Bible verses that accompanied it put to memory. But during one of his evangelistic conversations he realized he didn't actually have a personal relationship with Christ. Therefore, having grown up going to church and in a moral home, at the age of nineteen he repented of his sins, placed his faith in Jesus, and became a new creation. It was also during this time he felt God calling him to full-time vocational ministry.

Michael prepared for the ministry by going to seminary. In 1974, he married Terri, and the two of them soon had two daughters, Erin and Hayley. Throughout his adult life, he and Terri had conversations about how he never seemed to really "fit in" with his family. It wasn't an obsession or even a conspiracy theory; it was more like a splinter in his mind he shared only with Terri.

When they had these conversations, her response was, "Michael, if you were adopted, would it matter?" As far as he could tell, it wouldn't. He was secure in his identity in Christ, his calling as a pastor, and his relationship with his wife and two girls. The knowledge of adoption would only impact him by providing clarity to some lingering questions. Then one day the strangest—but strange only if you don't believe in the sovereignty of God—of occurrences took place.

Terri's mom was a local businesswoman who owned a flower shop. One day a lady who frequented the shop walked in and struck up a conversation, politely asking about Terri and how she was doing. It was a friendly conversation that in no way seemed out of the ordinary until Terri's mom mentioned her daughter had married a young man named Michael from

Pascagoula, Mississippi. The older woman said, "Oh, I know who he is! I handled his adoption!"

Michael's mother-in-law stumbled over her words for a moment and with a baffled look on her face said, "What?" The woman replied, "Yeah, I remember it clearly; I was a social worker and that was the first case I ever handled." She went on to describe Michael's family, affirming the type of details social workers typically know. When the seventy-year-old retiree left the shop, Terri received a call from her mother. They were both in shock. They contacted the woman again that same day to confirm her identity and get more information. The evidence left one conclusive verdict: Michael's occasional suspicions were, in fact, true.

This created a challenging situation for Terri: how and when—or even *if*—she should tell her husband. Following a lot of time in prayer seeking God's wisdom, she knew what to do. Terri and Michael took a trip during which he was to speak. It was also their wedding anniversary, so following the engagement, Michael took Terri out to a nice restaurant to celebrate. Over the course of the meal, Michael recalls "saying something about the adoption thing again." Terri responded, "Well, if you were adopted, would you want to know?" He responded in the affirmative and Terri proceeded to tell him.

At thirty-nine years of age, sitting in a restaurant in Kissimmee, Florida, Michael received clarity. He also felt an entirely different set of emotions than he could have ever anticipated. In that restaurant, time stood still, which is why he remembers the exact booth they were sitting in and all the cars in the parking lot. It was a defining moment.

In some strange way, clarity can serve as a gateway to confusion. Michael now knew he was adopted and thus had the truth at last. But why had his parents never told him? Why had his mother said things like, "Be careful, because cancer (or diabetes) runs in our family"?

Clarity is also not always accompanied by peace and satisfaction. This was certainly the case for Michael. He describes feeling frustrated, angry, and as if he had been punched in the gut. Michael went before the Lord in prayer and felt it wasn't best to approach his parents at the time, but he did speak to other people from his past. He called his former youth pastor, babysitter, and next-door neighbor, all of whom confirmed the fact that Michael having been adopted was common knowledge. This only fueled his anger, and an idea began to take hold in his mind: "I got a raw deal."

During this time, he escaped to a cabin in the mountains to get alone before God. Michael is a very spiritual man and knew peace could only come from above. A lot of raw and honest emotion burst out of him on this retreat, like the sudden arrival of a thunderstorm on a summer day. But Michael also says God began to reveal himself through his Word: In Isaiah 45 God stressed his sovereignty to Cyrus over and over again, saying, "I am the Lord, and there is no other" (verse 5). Verse 7 reads, "I form light and create darkness, I make well-being and create calamity, I am the Lord, who does all these things." Michael was shaken, and as he read on, the Word was like a sledgehammer, breaking to pieces the "I got a raw deal" mind-set that had begun to take root:

> *Woe to him who strives with him who formed him,*
> *a pot among earthen pots!*
> *Does the clay say to him who forms it, "What are you making?"*
> *or "Your work has no handles"?*

Woe to him who says to a father, "What are you begetting?"
or to a woman, "With what are you in labor?" (verses 9-10)

These verses brought Michael to his knees, to a point of surrender and desperation. He awakened to an idea he had preached many times: God works in ways I don't always understand. Michael returned from the mountain retreat confident that God was, in fact, the author of his circumstances.

Some time later, Michael's mother lay on her deathbed in an ICU. After years of praying, he decided to have an honest conversation with her about his adoption; one of their last conversations would be one of their most important. He was so grateful for the home and family she had given him and had completely forgiven her for never telling him the truth. Unfortunately, his dad would pass a short time later, before Michael could have that one last conversation.

Michael's was a story of confusion, clarity, more confusion, frustration, and surrender. But one question remains: What does this have to do with a redemptive imagination?

The central character of this story is actually Dr. Michael Catt, who serves as the pastor of Sherwood Baptist Church in Albany, Georgia. In recent years, the church has become known worldwide for the movies *Facing the Giants, Fireproof,* and most recently, *Courageous.* Sherwood Pictures, a ministry of the church, has reached millions through these Christian films, which have done quite well at the box office. Though Dr. Catt has demonstrated an incredible amount of gospel-centered creativity, that is not the point of this story.

Courageous is the story of four police officers tackling the most significant challenge of their lives: fatherhood. One of the main characters is Nathan Hayes, who grew up never meeting his biological father. Some influences along the way play a significant role in him becoming a man of God, and as a husband and father of two children, Nathan seems to be a case study of biblical manhood throughout the majority of the film. But in one of the final scenes, the audience realizes something is missing in his life; he has never forgiven his biological father for abandoning him. There is a poignant scene in which Nathan stands before his biological father's grave, prayerfully expressing forgiveness as he reads a letter to his father. Few people know the inspiration for that scene was Michael standing over his own father's grave.

ENGAGE

The manner in which Michael forgave his father is a beautiful portrait of a redemptive imagination at work. The Bible is clear on the subject of forgiveness:

- Jesus taught his disciples to pray, "Forgive us our debts, as we also have forgiven our debtors." He then commented on his own prayer by emphasizing forgiveness: "If you forgive others their trespasses, your heavenly Father will also forgive you, but if you do not forgive others their trespasses, neither will your Father forgive your trespasses" (Matthew 6:12,14-15).
- Paul teaches that part of being "chosen ones" means "bearing with one another and, if one has a complaint against another, forgiving each other; as the Lord has forgiven you, so you also must forgive" (Colossians 3:13).

Forgiveness is something we are to offer freely and frequently, but oftentimes the bridge between God's command and our obedience is a redemptive imagination. Michael's dad died before they could have a conversation, so he had to imagine another way. (It is important to understand that at this point there was no bitterness, just surrender.)

So much can change in such a short time. Where Michael was raised, adoption was a secret that wasn't to be shared, though in his case it seemed like everyone was keeping the secret from him. Today our thinking has progressed such that we celebrate the idea of adoption; some children grow up aware of it from an early age. Michael was aware of this cultural shift or progression but he still he needed to forgive, and the expression of forgiveness was part of his being obedient to the faith.

I have known Dr. Catt personally, as with so many characters in this book, for many years. The themes of surrender, desperation, and personal revival have always been evident in his preaching, writing, and producing. Evidence of this can be seen in the opening pages of *The Power of Desperation*, in which he wrote,

> Sometimes our loving Father has to orchestrate events to get our attention. He loves us, but will not leave us where he finds us. He waits patiently for our obedience, but if we do not pursue Him, He will pursue us. At various times along the journey, I have been frustrated with life, myself, and even with God. It wasn't until I learned the power of desperation that I was able to move into a new dimension of understanding.[1]

Redefine

- Keeping the first two plot movements in mind, what *ought not be* about the story of orphans in any society?
- Michael's story offers a wide array of complications, because it is littered with positive (example: Michael's parents adopting him) and negative (example: keeping this truth from him) aspects. Redefine his story in light of the four plot movements of Scripture.

Regain

- What is regained through the process of adoption? What does one declare *shall not be* with adoption?
- How was the theme of redemption limited? How did this aspect of the story fall short in reflecting the third plot movement?

Reimagine

- Even though Michael's story didn't exhaustively reflect the four plot movements, how did he restore by reimagining?
- Think of an example of a strained relationship you or someone you are close to may have. How can that relationship be restored by reimagining? How can a redemptive imagination be a bridge between what God has commanded and your obedience?

CHAPTER 15

DARK-HAIRED DARLING

Christina was a bright-eyed freshman, excited about high school and all the potential therein, when they met for the first time. She had come from a prominent Christian family that instilled within her a biblical worldview and desire for the things of God. Her roots were Italian on her mother's side, a family that had come to the States just two generations earlier. Her father, like so many Americans, had a bit of diversity running throughout his family tree. Hers was an enchanted childhood filled with incredible memories guided by parents who love Jesus.

As she grew, Christina, like so many young girls, dreamed of finding her own Prince Charming—and all the fairy-tale notions that accompany such a desired goal. Armed with a quick wit from her father and accompanied by a dark-haired Italian look from her mother, she entered into the vast unknown world called "high school."

He was a senior finishing his high school journey when they met. His family had immigrated from Puerto Rico and from all indications seemed to have a deep commitment to the things of God. It didn't take long for their paths to meet, and it didn't take long after that for them to fall in love. Unlike most young ladies who seem to fall in and out of love a few times throughout high school, and unlike most young men who seem to fall in and out of love every other day, theirs was a relationship that enjoyed an incredible amount of tenure.

They would spend the next four years dating, spending their weekends at church activities with their friends and parents. It seemed to be a healthy relationship that honored the Lord and the homes from whence they both came. Therefore, it was no surprise that they would marry at a young age, she after a year of college at nineteen and he at twenty-three. It was a matrimony full of potential and hope. She had grown up on mission, and he had demonstrated on more than one occasion a willingness to make big sacrifices in order to serve those less fortunate. Marriage made perfect sense and seemed to be an open door of opportunity for a daring adventure serving God. At the wedding no expense was spared; the guest list read as a who's who for a certain segment of evangelicalism in America. Her father gave her away, and the two exchanged vows and dashed away for a honeymoon at an expensive resort in a tropical location.

For the previous five years, everything had seemed to be picture-perfect, but five minutes after the honeymoon, Prince Charming and the fairy tale were more of a distant memory than a present reality. Nevertheless, Christina pressed on.

Both were accepted as transfers to an Ivy League school, which took them far from their central Florida home. There his love for her became as cold as the Boston winter outside.

At first, he simply appeared to be distant and uncaring. By the end, he was unfaithful, abusive, and had abandoned her on more than one occasion. Once, while they were visiting family, he abandoned her over 1,300 miles away from their home in Boston. Another time he took away her key and locked her out in the cold. Two policemen had to help her break into her own apartment. More than once, she caught him with pornography, and the evidence for infidelity was so strong that she had to be tested for STDs. The abuse was verbal and psychological rather than physical; nevertheless, his mistreatment of her would leave wounds that would take some time to heal.

Christina dedicated herself to finishing her degree and salvaging some part of this horrific chapter in her life. Absent of relational certainty, she pressed on day after day, focused on the task at hand: studies and graduation. Then one day while she was crossing the street, a young man accidentally ran a red light and struck her with his car. The accident left her hospitalized for a short time and then required her to see a specialist for months, all while she was trying to finish college.

She missed graduating with honors by a tenth of a point. On graduation day she received a college diploma—with the ink still drying on divorce papers and a headache that would come and go for years after the accident. Most would feel a sense of accomplishment and optimism about the future at the age of twenty-one, having just graduated from an Ivy League school, but not Christina and not this day. Any sense of accomplishment had been replaced with a sense of failure, shame, and guilt. As a divorced daughter of a Baptist preacher, she felt as if she had shamed her family, her church, her Christian teachers, and, most important, Jesus. When life was supposed to be just beginning, she felt as if it were already over.

Following graduation and the divorce, she moved back into her old room where she found safe haven from the outside world. There Christina locked herself away. Her loneliness was the penance she paid for the guilt she felt. Hope had faded away and with it the faith that there could ever be better days. This, for now, was as good as it got.

And then her mother interrupted the sadness. She signed Christina up for a young-adult trip to the beach that a church in the area was taking and bought her some new clothes and a bathing suit. This seemingly small step helped Christina make great progress. While at the retreat, one of the pastors introduced her to several people who befriended her almost immediately. Before long, she was heavily involved in the church and even entertaining thoughts about a new kind of normal.

The first time I saw her was at a student conference in Orlando. She was there just to help out for the week, and I was a youth pastor attending with my students. I often joke that the way we met was when I walked up to her and said, "Hello, my name is Will . . . God's will." With lines like that, how could she resist? However, the actual manner of our meeting was more spiritual than that. Christina had taken an interest in a young lady in our group who didn't quite fit in, a feeling someone should never have in our church settings. Little did she know that such a decision would completely change the trajectory of both of our lives. For the better part of the week, we spent time together and enjoyed one of those instant connections. One night we decided to go out for a cup of coffee. Halfway through the evening, I grabbed her hand and we danced to a song I hummed. That night we danced, and we haven't let go of each other since.

You see, this idea of redemptive imagination is very personal to me. I wake up every day, and when I look at my wife, I realize that I am the beneficiary of how God's grace can help us reimagine our lives. On our third date, I told her I would one day marry her; within six months we were engaged; and within a year from when we met, we were husband and wife. Ten years of marriage has produced three children, more ministry opportunities and memories than I can count, and a deeper love for each other than I ever knew existed.

Christina went on to get a master's degree in biblical counseling, a skill set that has served her well through the years, counseling young ladies who wouldn't have otherwise been able to afford it. She has managed our household, started a nonprofit ministry, helped me write two books, and tirelessly aided me through two master's degrees and a PhD. She is Proverbs 31 and a cross between rock and roll and Martha Stewart. And yet most of what you have just read, she would tell you, feels like a lifetime ago. She still remembers it in her head, but the pain of it is no longer felt in her heart—something only God's love for his daughter could accomplish. God has not erased her memories, but he has healed them and allowed her to redemptively reimagine a new life.

CHAPTER 16

THE CHALLENGE

So here is to the dreamers of the day
those redeemed renegades who dare to look out a different window
those who refuse to believe that the present situation is "as good as
*   it gets"*
go on, dreamers of the day, with your conscious dreams
your imaginary thoughts about real things
go on and imagine how it could and should be
go on in the name of God under the banner of his redemption
find solutions where others only found problems
help the hopeless with an enduring conviction that the redeemed are
*   not helpless*
open doors that have been closed and kept shut by closed minds
rebuild walls when many have grown comfortable with the routine of
*   rubble*
ask the questions no one is willing to ask
seek the answers that have been long lost due to stalled
*   imaginations*

be fully human in a world that increasingly devalues human life
turn a thought into a revolution and a wild hair into a
    wonderful life
go on, dreamers of the day, as if the sun were setting and your time
    is now or never
pick up your million-to-one ideas realizing God never played the odds
let your visions and ideas find there infinite possibilities in a reflec-
    tion of the One who is infinitely creative
refuse the comfort of conformity and pathetic outcome of pessimistic
    thinking
carry the torch of your idea if you be the only one
your flash of genius will not go unnoticed
unleash your courageous ponderings as if someone's life depended
    upon their actualization
take action, initiate, as if your life depended upon it
become intoxicated by your redemptive imagination
may you only find rest when you slip away to slumber
may the imaginations in the day only be interrupted by the dreams
    of the night
militantly refuse to compromise while at the same time be branded
    by the compassionate nature of your imagination
oh, dreamers of the day, carry on until it is carried out
catch a fire and set the problem ablaze with your redemptive
    imagination
not because you can . . . but because you must
because grace demands more and never less
because the redeemed never take a time out
because the mission of God leaves you no other option
choose this because you have been chosen
motivated not by problem or even the solution first

*but rather be supremely motivated by the position granted you by
    the grace of God
go on, dreamers of the day, with your redemptive imaginations
because you live at the feet of Jesus*

ACKNOWLEDGMENTS

Trying to narrow down my acknowledgments to fit on this page has been a tough task because so many have contributed to and shaped my thinking concerning imagination and the glory of God. For this I am forever grateful to all who have taken the time to tell and retell me stories, engaging my imagination over the years. I want to give a special thanks to "Pop," as I remember my first experience with imagination as a child sitting on his living room floor while he drew with his finger the outline of his base camp from the war. By the time he was done, my imagination had come alive in such a way that the living room had been transformed before my very eyes.

I also want to thank those whose stories have helped make this project a reality: Dale Glover, Nancy Hunter Harrell, Dr. Michael Catt, Open Baptist Church and Face the Nation, Coach Kris Hogan and Faith Christian School, and my dad, who is a continual stroke of inspiration.

I want to express my deep appreciation to those who taught me that the grand story God has told is the story that determines all other stories: my parents Roy and Karen Crowe, Dr. Jay Strack, Dr. Daniel Akin, Dr. Bruce Ashford, Dr. Alvin Reid, and Dr. Bill Brown. Additionally, thank you to the tens of thousands of students who have attended Student Leadership University and are answering the dangerous question *What would I do if I knew I would not fail?*

To my children, whose imaginations serve as a wardrobe into other worlds, thanks for letting me join in the journey to distant lands and magical places. And, lastly, to my wife, Christina, imagining what we could do for the glory of God is the adventure of a lifetime.

NOTES

Introduction: Redemptive Imagination and the Two Wills of God

1. Wayne Grudem, *Systematic Theology* (Grand Rapids, MI: Zondervan, 1994), 216–217.
2. John Piper, "Are There Two Wills in God?" *Desiring God Blog*, January 1, 1995, http://www.desiringgod.org/resource-library/articles/are-there-two-wills-in-god.
3. Daniel Akin, "A Great Commission Theology for Life," February 19, 2009, http://www.danielakin.com/wp-content/uploads/2009/02/1-timothy-21-7-a-great-commission-theology-for-life-outlineand-manuscript-ds.pdf.
4. C. S. Lewis, *God in the Dock* (London: Curtis Brown, 1944), 66–67.
5. Gene Edward Veith Jr., *God at Work* (Wheaton, IL: Crossway, 2002), 19.

Chapter 1: Imaginology: The Scaffolding for Imaginary Thoughts

1. "William R. 'Bill' Bright, Founder of World's Largest Christian Ministry Dies," BillBright.com, July 19, 2003, http://billbright.ccci.org/public.
2. J. I. Packer, *Knowing God* (Downers Grove, IL: InterVarsity, 1973), 19.

3. Alister E. McGrath, *Christian Theology* (Oxford: Blackwell Publishing, 2007), 121.
4. McGrath, 121.
5. McGrath, 136.
6. McGrath, 141.
7. McGrath, 145.
8. The *supreme norm* is a phrase used by Dr. Bruce Ashford, dean of the College at Southeastern Baptist Theological Seminary in Wake Forest, North Carolina.
9. Bruce R. Ashford, ed., *Theology and Practice of Mission* (Nashville: B&H Academic, 2011), 6–7.
10. Warren W. Wiersbe, *Preaching and Teaching with Imagination* (Grand Rapids, MI: Baker, 1994), 24.
11. W. MacNeile Dixon, *The Human Situation*, in Wiersbe, 24.
12. Brian Godawa, *Hollywood Worldviews: Watching Films with Wisdom and Discernment* (Downers Grove, IL: InterVarsity, 2002), 10.
13. Godawa, 27.
14. Quote compiled from C. S. Lewis, *Mere Christianity* (New York: Touchstone, 1996), 109–112.
15. Ashford, 13.
16. Adapted from the original title of John Bunyan's classic *The Pilgrim's Progress from This World to That Which Is to Come*.
17. Ashford, 15.

Chapter 2: The Rise and Fall of Christian Imagination

1. Francis A. Schaeffer, *How Should We Then Live?* (Wheaton, IL: Crossway, 1983), 19.
2. Schaeffer, 20.
3. Alvin J. Schmidt, *How Christianity Changed the World* (Grand Rapids, MI: Zondervan, 2004), 49.
4. Schmidt, 49.
5. Schmidt, 52.
6. Schmidt, 53.
7. Schmidt, 61.
8. Summarized from two sources: Charles Colson, *Loving God* (Grand Rapids, MI: Zondervan, 1997), 241–243, and

P. Schaff and H. Wace, eds., *A Select Library of the Nicene and Post-Nicene Fathers of the Christian Church, Second Series, Volume 3: Theodoret, Jerome, Gennadius, Rufinus: Historial Writings, etc.* (New York: Christian Literature Company, 1892), 151.

9. P. L. Tan, *Encyclopedia of 7700 Illustrations: A Treasury of Illustrations, Anecdotes, Facts and Quotations for Pastors, Teachers and Christian Workers* (Garland, TX: Bible Communications, 1996), e-book, 916.

10. Francis Gerald Ensley, *John Wesley: Evangelist* (Nashville: Methodist Evangelistic Materials, 1958), 7.

11. Tan, 918.

12. Tan, 918.

13. J. C. Ryle, *Christian Leaders of the Eighteenth Century* (Carlisle, England: The Banner of Truth Trust, 1978), 80.

14. Ryle, 80.

15. *Selected Letters of John Wesley*, ed. Frederick C. Gill (New York: Philosophical Library, 1956), 237.

16. Kevin Belmonte, *Hero for Humanity* (Colorado Springs, CO: NavPress, 2002), 102.

17. Summarized from Belmonte.

18. Summarized from June Rose, *Elizabeth Fry* (New York: St. Martin's Press, 1980), and Mark Galli and Ted Olsen, eds., *131 Christians Everyone Should Know* (Nashville: Broadman, Holman, 2000), 286–287.

19. Rose, xiii.

20. "Orphans," UNICEF.org, May 25, 2012, http://www.unicef.org/media/media_45279.html.

21. "Global Report on Trafficking in Persons," United Nations Office on Drugs and Crime, February 2009, http://www.unodc.org/documents/human-trafficking/Global_Report_on_TIP.pdf.

22. Sugam Pokharel, "U.S States of Play in Anti-Trafficking Laws," The Facts — The CNN Freedom Project: Ending Modern-Day Slavery, August 8, 2012, http://thecnnfreedomproject.blogs.cnn.com/category/the-facts.

23. "Hunger Stats," World Food Programme, accessed August 20, 2012, http://www.wfp.org/hunger/stats.

24. Shane Claiborne, "Imagine a New World," *Reject Apathy*, no. 1, Spring 2012, http://rejectapathy.com/magazine/archives/issue-01/statements/25468-imagine-a-new-world.

25. Claiborne, 16.

26. Claiborne, 16.

Chapter 3: A New Kind of Normal: Activating a Redemptive Imagination

1. Warren W. Wiersbe, *Preaching and Teaching with Imagination* (Grand Rapids, MI: Baker, 1994), 24–25.

2. Wiersbe, 27.

3. W. Ian Thomas, *The Indwelling Life of Christ* (Sisters, OR: Multnomah, 2006), 70.

4. Charles R. Swindoll, *The Tale of the Tardy Oxcart* (Nashville: Word, 1998), 453.

5. E. Stanley Jones, in Swindoll, 453.

6. John Bunyan, in Swindoll, 452.

7. Wiersbe, 29.

8. Robert S. Stern, "Benefits of Moderate Sun Exposure," *Harvard Medical School Family Health Guide*, June 2004, http://www.health.harvard.edu/fhg/updates/update0604d.shtml.

9. Stern.

Chapter 4: Dreaming with the Lights On: Applying a Redemptive Imagination

1. John C. Maxwell, *Today Matters* (New York: Warner Faith, 2004), xi.

2. Kalle Lasn, *Culture Jam: The Uncooling of America* (New York: Eagle Brook, 1999), xiii.

3. R. Jamieson, A. R. Fausset, and D. Brown, *A Commentary, Critical and Explanatory, on the Old and New Testaments* (Eph. 3:20) (Oak Harbor, WA: Logos Research Systems, 1997).

4. R. R. Melick Jr., *Vol. 32: Philippians, Colossians, Philemon*, The New American Commentary (Nashville: Broadman, Holman, 2001), electronic ed., 154.

5. Melick.

6. Justo L. González, *The Story of Christianity*, vol. 1 (San Francisco: HarperCollins, 1984), 319–321.

Chapter 5: When Daddy Sang

1. Dave Helton, "The Ship Captain Who Missed His Boyhood," *Houston Press*, July 7, 1961.
2. Warren Wiersbe, ed., *The Best of A. W. Tozer* (Harrisburg, PA: Christian Publications, 1978), 14.
3. Wiersbe, 17.
4. "C. S. Lewis on Myth," Don King's Literature Page at Montreat College, accessed June 23, 2012, http://ww2.montreat.edu/dking/lewis/MYTH.htm.

Chapter 6: Creativity and a Different Kind of Crazy

1. *The Free Dictionary*, s.v. "disorder," accessed June 23, 2012, http://medical-dictionary.thefreedictionary.com/Mental+disability.
2. John Calvin, "The Corinthians," in *Calvin's Commentaries*, vol. 20 (Grand Rapids, MI: Baker, 2005), 411.

Chapter 7: Friday Night and the Light of Jesus

1. Rick Reilly, "There Are Some Games in Which Cheering for the Other Side Feels Better Than Winning," Life of Reilly, *ESPN Magazine*, December 12, 2008, http://sports.espn.go.com/espnmag/story?section=magazine&id=3789373.
2. "One Heart: The Beginning of a Movement," Film Associates of OneHeart, accessed August 20, 2012, http://www.oneheartmovie.com/ohp.html.
3. "A Powerful Sports Drama," Film Associates of OneHeart, accessed August 20, 2012, http://www.oneheartmovie.com/index.html.
4. Reilly.
5. David Ferguson, *The Great Commandment Principle* (Wheaton, IL: Tyndale, 1998), 7.

Chapter 8: Face the Nation

1. Robert I. Rotberg, *Botswana* (Philadelphia: Mason Crest Publishers, 2008), 58.
2. Robert Guest, *The Shackled Continent* (London: Pan Books, 2005), 90.
3. "About FTN," Face the Nation: Reaching Botswana for Christ, accessed June 23, 2012, http://facethenation.org/blog/about-ftn.
4. Modise Mokgwathise, "Forward," *OB Server*, no. 14, October 2010.
5. W. A. Elwell and P. W. Comfort, *Tyndale Bible Dictionary* (Wheaton, IL: Tyndale, 2001), 387.
6. Elwell and Comfort, 387.

Chapter 9: A Father Imagines Forgiveness

1. J. M. Freeman and H. J. Chadwick, *Manners and Customs of the Bible*, rev. ed. (North Brunswick, NJ: Bridge-Logos Publishers, 1998), 444.
2. W. Barclay, ed., *The Gospel of Matthew: Volume 2, The Daily Study Bible*, rev. ed. (Philadelphia: Westminster, 2002).
3. Walter Hooper, ed., *Letters of C. S. Lewis* (New York: MacMillan, 1979), 255.

Chapter 10: The Day the Bullied Died

1. "Bullying Today," The Bully Project, accessed June 23, 2012, http://thebullyproject.com/indexflash.html#/bullyingtoday.
2. Martin Luther, "Concerning Christian Liberty," *The Harvard Classics*, vol. 36, part 6 (New York: Collier, 1909–1914); see also "Concerning Christian Liberty," Bartleby.com, accessed June 23, 2012, http://www.bartleby.com/36/6/2.html.
3. Luther.

Chapter 11: A Stroke of Inspiration

1. W. Ian Thomas, *The Indwelling Life of Christ* (Sisters, OR: Multnomah, 2006), 54.
2. Thomas, 55.
3. Matthew Henry, *Matthew Henry's Commentary on the Whole Bible* (Is. 45:5-10) (Peabody, MA: Hendrickson, 1996).

4. C. F. Pfeiffer, *The Wycliffe Bible Commentary: Old Testament* (Is. 45:7) (Chicago: Moody, 1962).

Chapter 12: Lord Save the Country Boy
1. Daniel Akin, "A Great Commission Theology for Life," accessed 23 June 2012, http://www.danielakin.com/ wp-content/uploads/2009/02/1-timothy-21-7-a-great -commission-theology-for-life-outlineand-manuscript-ds.pdf, 2009.
2. Christopher J. H. Wright, *The Mission of God* (Downers Grove, IL: IVP Academic, 2006), 23.
3. Wright, 31.

Chapter 13: Boys Who Shave
1. John MacArthur, "Ephesians," in *The MacArthur New Testament Commentary* (Chicago: Moody, 1986), 319.
2. Robin Marantz Henig, "What Is It About 20-Somethings?" *New York Times Magazine,* August 18, 2010, http://www .nytimes.com/2010/08/22/magazine/22Adulthood-t .html?pagewanted=all.
3. Darrin Patrick, *Church Planter* (Wheaton, IL: Crossway, 2010), 9.

Chapter 14: A Courageous Imagination
1. Michael Catt, *The Power of Desperation* (Nashville: Broadman, Holman, 2009), 2.

ABOUT THE AUTHOR

BRENT CROWE is a thought-provoking visionary and speaker who engages such issues as leadership, culture, and change. He speaks to tens of thousands across the nation and abroad each year and is currently serving as vice president for Student Leadership University, a program that has trained more than fifty thousand students to commit themselves to excellence.

Brent is married to Christina and they have three children: Gabriel, Charis, and Mercy. He is a PhD candidate and holds two master's degrees (an MDiv in evangelism and an MA in ethics) from Southeastern Baptist Theological Seminary. His other works include *IMPACT: Student Leadership Bible*, *The Call*, and most recently *Chasing Elephants*.

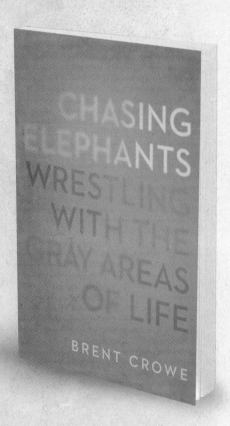